PENGUIN
COMPASS

LIVE IN A BETTER WAY

His Holiness the Dalai Lama, the exiled religious and temporal leader of Tibet and winner of the 1989 Nobel Peace Prize, is recognized internationally as a spiritual leader and peace statesman. He lives in Dharamsala, India.

Lama Thubten Zopa Rinpoche is the inspiring spiritual director of the Foundation for the Preservation of the Mahayana Tradition, a worldwide Tibetan Buddhist organization.

Renuka Singh is an Associate Professor at Jawaharlal Nehru University in New Delhi, India. She compiled and edited *The Path to Tranquility,* by her spiritual teacher His Holiness the Dalai Lama.

His Holiness the Dalai Lama

LIVE
IN A
BETTER
WAY

Reflections on
Truth, Love,
and
Happiness

COMPILED AND EDITED BY
Renuka Singh

PENGUIN COMPASS

PENGUIN COMPASS
Published by the Penguin Group
Penguin Putnam Inc., 375 Hudson Street,
New York, New York 10014, U.S.A.
Penguin Books Ltd, 80 Strand, London WC2R 0RL, England
Penguin Books Australia Ltd, 250 Camberwell Road,
Camberwell, Victoria 3124, Australia
Penguin Books Canada Ltd, 10 Alcorn Avenue,
Toronto, Ontario, Canada M4V 3B2
Penguin Books India (P) Ltd, 11 Community Centre,
Panchsheel Park, New Delhi - 110 017, India
Penguin Books (N.Z.) Ltd, Cnr Rosedale and Airborne Roads,
Albany, Auckland, New Zealand
Penguin Books (South Africa) (Pty) Ltd, 24 Sturdee Avenue,
Rosebank, Johannesburg 2196, South Africa

Penguin Books Ltd, Registered Offices:
Harmondsworth, Middlesex, England

First published in India under the title
The Transformed Mind by Penguin Books India 1999
First published in the United States of America by
Viking Compass, a member of Penguin Putnam Inc. 2001
Published in Penguin Compass 2002

1 3 5 7 9 10 8 6 4 2

THE LIBRARY OF CONGRESS HAS CATALOGED
THE AMERICAN HARDCOVER EDITION AS FOLLOWS:
Bstan-'dzin-rgya-mtsho, Dali Lama XIV, 1935–
Live in a Better Way/ Reflections of Truth, Love and Happiness/
Compiled and Edited by Renuka Singh with a Practical Introduction
to Buddhism by Lama Thubten Zopa Rinpoche
p. cm.
Includes index.
ISBN 0-670-89671-3 (hc.)
ISBN 0 14 21.9607 X (pbk.)
1. Spiritual life—Buddhism. I. Singh, Renuka, 1953– II. Title
BQ7935.B774 L58 2001
294.3'444—dc21   00-043700

Printed in the United States of America
Set in Perpetua • Designed by Francesca Belanger

CONTENTS

EDITOR'S NOTE

THIS BOOK is a compilation of selected lectures delivered by His Holiness the Dalai Lama at Tushita's dharma celebrations held annually in New Delhi. It includes as well an illuminating foreword by Venerable Lama Thubten Zopa Rinpoche. I am honored that His Holiness and Rinpoche have permitted me this opportunity to bring together this distinctive series of lectures that emphasize the importance of spirituality in a world now dominated by an ethos of scientific and technological rationality. His Holiness offers a clear and penetrating insight into the problems facing mankind and how love, compassion and universal responsibility are required to skillfully solve these problems.

To commemorate the twentieth anniversary of Tushita Mahayana Meditation Centre, founded in 1979 by the late Lama Yeshe and Lama Zopa Rinpoche, I would like to offer this book to His Holiness as a token of our gratitude for his immeasurable kindness. I would also like to offer this book—as we start the new millennium—to a wider audience as a guide for their practice of meditation in order that they can transform their minds and achieve Enlightenment. Indeed, the basic purpose of reading and listening to the Buddhist teachings is to equip ourselves with tools of understanding so that we can engage in the proper kind of "spiritual combat."

The lectures follow a chronological order of events except the last discourse on the Two Truths, which was delivered over two consecutive evenings in 1988. His Holiness often refers to the Two Truths and Four Noble Truths in the other lectures in this collection that deal with, for example, the issues of transforming one's mind; of the journey to happiness by understanding the suffering nature of cyclic existence and the realization of emptiness; of solving personal, national and international problems with compassion and nonviolence; of how to live and die in a better way; and of the path for spiritual practice through renunciation, *bodhicitta* and the wisdom of emptiness—this being the essence of the dharma that effectively liberates all beings. Hence, for conceptual and philosophical clarity, it seemed more appropriate to place this discourse on the Two Truths at the end, reflecting on their profundity and complexity.

I have also included here most of the question and answer sessions that followed the lectures. Most of the questions were taken from the audience. I have tried to avoid repetition wherever possible, yet due to the nature of the discourses, certain mistakes might have crept in as a result of transcription or misinterpretation.

Many individuals have made significant contributions toward the success of this endeavor. I am deeply indebted to such lovable and revered teachers as His Holiness the Dalai Lama and Venerable Lama Thubten Zopa Rinpoche for their kindness and inspiration. A very special thanks to Venerable Lhakdor-la for taking out time to correct the manuscript (in Dharamsala, on the plane and in the United States) and for being the translator for our talks. I would like to express my appreciation to Thubten Jimpa-la as well for translating the lecture delivered in 1997. I am always grateful to Tenzin Geyche Tethong-la, private secretary to His Holiness, for putting up with my demands and for all his help and cooperation.

Had it not been for the diligence and joyous involvement of all my predecessors and spiritual program coordinators, Tushita would not have been what it is today. Support from all our generous sponsors, friends, members and the Foundation for the Preservation of Mahayana Tradition has helped Tushita survive all these years. To name a few, the Kakarias, Mathurs, Roys, Khannas, Bhandaris, Nandas, Suds, Cerris, Chawlas, Jhalanis, Singhs, Venerable Yeshe Chodron, Susie Roy, Bruno Furrer, Derek Goh and Joan Mahony have been great pillars of strength. I would also like to mention the important role played by Venerable Marcel Bertels, Venerable Roger Kunsang and Dr. Nick Ribush in the history of Tushita. A heartfelt thanks for their patience, help and commitment.

Assistance from Karthika and Diya Kar Hazra at Penguin has been fruitful in giving this book its final form. I thank them for working tirelessly.

Last but not the least, I would like to express my gratitude to my family for being a constant source of encouragement and affection. I miss especially the love and support of my late sister Ashma Singh, who was a fellow traveler with me in the spiritual pursuit and quietly contributed a great deal to the activities of Tushita.

May this book deepen the spiritual understanding and experience of many people and bring peace in their lives.

Renuka Singh
New Delhi
November 1999

INTRODUCTION

In 1976, my precious teacher, the late Lama Thubten Yeshe (1935–84), who was kinder than the Buddhas of the past, present and future, decided to establish a Buddhist center in Delhi to help repay the kindness of the Indian people in providing the dharma to Tibet.

As everybody knows, Guru Shākyamuni Buddha, the founder of the dharma we enjoy today, was born in northern India (now Lumbini, Nepal) over twenty-five hundred years ago. His father was king of the powerful Sākya clan. At the age of twenty-nine, his son and heir, Prince Siddhārtha Gautama, motivated by the wish to understand why suffering exists and how, if at all, it can be overcome, renounced the kingdom and left the palace in search of the true nature of all existence. After studying for six years with many great Hindu teachers and engaging in many austere practices that led him to almost die from malnutrition, Prince Siddhārtha decided to follow the middle path between the extremes of the overindulgence of his former palace life and the self-mortification of his more recent practices. Thus, at what is now Buddh Gaya, Bihar, he sat beneath the bodhi tree and meditated in solitude until he realized his goal: complete, full, unparalleled Enlightenment. Thus he became Lord Shākyamuni Buddha, the enlightened sage of the Sākya clan.

For almost half a century he led the homeless life of a renunciate, wandering from place to place preaching, and spending almost every summer in retreat. His first lessons were given at Sarnath, about seven weeks after his Enlightenment. Here he gave his famous discourse on the Four Noble Truths, in which he explained that the nature of worldly life is suffering, that this suffering has a cause, that this suffering can cease completely and that there is a path to this cessation. Subsequently, wherever he went, he taught those who were receptive whatever they needed to know, according to their level of mind. Thus, over the course of his lifetime, and in no particular order, the Buddha imparted an incredible amount of deep and vast knowledge to a huge number of people. Finally, at Kushinagar, at the age of eighty, he passed away. His final words were that since all conditioned phenomena are impermanent, we should not be attached to anything, but should instead exert ourselves diligently to avoid evil, do only good and purify our minds. This, in essence, was the teaching of the Buddha.

Over the next thousand years, Buddhism—the dharma, the teachings of the Buddha—flourished in India and spread to many other countries like Sri Lanka, Pakistan, Afghanistan, Burma, Nepal, Thailand and other Southeast Asian countries, China, Korea and Japan. Broadly, Buddhism developed into two main schools; the principal difference between the two is defined more by the motivation of the practitioner than by any outer form. In general, however, the Hinayana school established itself and was found in southern countries, while the Mahayana school spread north.

In the early part of the seventh century A.D., the king of Tibet, Songtsen Gampo (617–50), married two Buddhist princesses, one from Nepal, the other from China. Through their influence, he became a Buddhist, and he sowed the seeds of Buddhism in Tibet by building several temples and sending one of his ministers, Thönmi Sambhota, to India to create a written script so that Buddhist texts could be translated from

Sanskrit into Tibetan. About a hundred years later, one of his successors, Trisong Detsen (742–97), invited the great Indian teachers Shantarakshita and Padmasambhava to Tibet. Thus, despite many ups and downs, over the next several centuries, Buddhism spread throughout Tibet. However, at the beginning of the eleventh century, Tibetan Buddhism was in serious decline, with false and misleading teachings coming to the fore and degenerate practices becoming rampant everywhere. Dismayed by all this, King Lhalama Yeshe Ö of Gu-ge, in the far west of Tibet, invited the great Indian scholar-saint Atīśa (982–1054) to Tibet to reintroduce the pure dharma to the Land of Snows.

Like Guru Shākyamuni Buddha, Atīśa too was born into a royal family but forsook his kingdom in Bengal in favor of the spiritual life. During his teens and twenties he undertook deep study and practice of sutra and tantra, and just before turning thirty, was ordained as a monk and given the name Dīpankara. His heart was set upon attaining Enlightenment, and his many experiences impressed upon him the importance of developing *bodhicitta* as its principal cause. He discovered that the greatest contemporary teacher of *bodhicitta* was the renowned Guru Suvarnadvipi, who lived in what is probably now Sumatra. Atīśa, therefore, undertook an extremely hazardous and arduous thirteen-month journey across the ocean to study under this great teacher. He remained with him for twelve years, studying and practicing until he developed *bodhicitta*. He then returned to India and eventually took up residence at the great monastic university of Vikramasila in Magadha. It was there that Lhalama Yeshe Ö's emissaries found Atīśa and begged him to go to Tibet.

Since Atīśa was one of the greatest scholars in India, the abbot of Vikramasila was reluctant to give him permission to go to Tibet, but eventually he agreed to let him go for a period of three years. By this time, King Lhalama Yeshe Ö had died and his nephew Jangchub Ö was king. When Atīśa arrived, Jangchub Ö explained how seriously the dharma had declined in Tibet. He beseeched Atīśa to teach not the most profound and amazing teachings, but rather the law of cause and effect and some unmistaken dharma that was easy to practice and encompassed the entire teaching of the Enlightened One.

Extremely pleased, Atīśa thereupon composed a short, three-page text entitled *A Lamp for the Path to Enlightenment,* which clarified both the

sutra and tantra teachings of the Buddha. Soon after this, the erroneous teachings that had so
plagued Tibet completely disappeared, and the
pure dharma spread far and wide. This was
greatly fortunate not only for the people of Tibet
but for the world at large. During this period,
Buddhism in India was under siege from the destructive forces that had invaded the country
from the west, razing monasteries to the ground,
killing monks and burning texts. The dharma
never recovered from this assault and over the
next thousand years all but disappeared from India, the land of its birth. It was the preservation
of the complete form of Mahayana Buddhism that
had been brought to Tibet and that guaranteed its
continued existence for all mankind.

The short text that Atīsa had composed was the
first in a body of teachings that came to be called,
in Tibetan, "*Lam-rim,*" or the "steps of the path to
Enlightenment." *The Lam-rim* teachings do not
contain anything that was not taught by the Buddha himself. Rather, they are simply an arrange-
ment of everything the Buddha taught over
forty-five years in a coherent and logical framework that allows any individual to see clearly how
he or she should follow the path. The *Lam-rim* is
essentially a map to the full Enlightenment of

Buddhahood. Atīśa's followers further developed this unique presentation of the dharma, and the *Lam-rim* teachings became the foundation for most of the Tibetan schools of Buddhism that developed over the following centuries. Their own school became known as the *Kadam* tradition.

Not only did Atīśa introduce to his followers the *Lam-rim* but he also brought with him both the wisdom and method lineages of Lord Buddha's teachings. Shākyamuni Buddha transmitted his wisdom teachings to Manjushri, who passed them on to the incomparable Indian pundit and yogi Nagarjuna, and thence to Chandrakirti and many other great scholars down the centuries to Atīśa. The method teachings were transmitted to Maitreya, who passed them on through many teachers such as Asanga, Vasubandhu and Suvarnadvipi, from whom they also reached Atīśa. Thus the teachings that Atīśa brought to Tibet were not only the pure teachings of the Buddha but they had also been transmitted through an unbroken lineage that could be traced back to Guru Shākyamuni himself. This unsullied oral tradition was maintained in Tibet and still exists today in the minds of great lamas like His Holiness the Dalai Lama, from whom we are able to receive it.

In the fifteenth century Tibet saw a great teacher in Lama Tsong Khapa (1357–1419). Greatly influenced by the *Kadampas* and having studied with famous masters from the three main traditions of the time—the *Nyingma, Kagyu* and *Sākya*—Lama Tsong Khapa founded a new tradition, the *Gelug,* which soon became the prevalent school of Buddhism in Tibet. This is the school to which the Dalai Lamas would come to belong and the one we follow at Tushita Mahayana Meditation Centre.

I mentioned earlier that there are two main schools of Buddhism in general: the Hinayana and the Mahayana. The Mahayana is further divided into Paramitayana and Vajrayana, which are also known as Sutrayana and Tantrayana respectively. I also mentioned that the main difference between Hinayana and Mahayana lies in the motivation of their practitioners. This can be summarized by a quotation from His Holiness the Dalai Lama: "The practice of Buddhism can be summarized in the short phrase 'If you can't help others, at least don't harm them.'" This reflects the motivation that distinguishes the two main Buddhist schools from each other. Ideally, practitioners should dedicate their activities to helping others in the highest way possible, that is, by leading them to

Enlightenment. This is the Mahayana motivation: to strive for Enlightenment for the sake of all sentient beings. The term for this mind of ultimate altruism is *"bodhicitta,"* and Atīśa's dangerous journey and years of practice in search of its realization underscore its importance. Those unable to generate such extensive motivation are exhorted to at least not do harm to others, and this is the basis of Hinayana practice: to follow the path of ahimsa (nonviolence) and to strive for individual liberation from suffering—moksha or nirvana. It should perhaps be stressed, however, that these fundamental practices also underlie the practice of both divisions of the Mahayana.

Since the Sutrayana and Tantrayana are Mahayana schools, the motivation of practitioners of both is obviously *bodhicitta*: the attainment of Enlightenment for the sole purpose of enlightening all others. The difference between them is the speed with which this goal can be accomplished. Practitioners of the sutra path may take countless eons to become enlightened; by practicing the special profound techniques of tantra it can be done in just a few years or a few lifetimes. All these Buddhist traditions—Hinayana, Sutrayana and Tantrayana—originated in India and were transmitted to Tibet, where they were preserved, practiced and developed to the full in the uniquely isolated and conducive atmosphere of Tibet.

Everything changed, of course, when the Chinese Communists began to occupy Tibet soon after they came to power in China in 1949, and reached a critical point in 1959, when the Tibetan people rose up against their oppressors but were ruthlessly put down. His Holiness the Dalai Lama, his family and many of his teachers fled the murderous rage of the People's Liberation Army to safety in India, along with some one hundred thousand other Tibetans. I myself, although born in Nepal and had studied at a monastery in southern Tibet, was part of this exodus. Allowing us a safe haven from persecution and likely death at this crucial time was another of India's great kindnesses to the Tibetan people.

Thus it was that Lama Yeshe felt a need to try to repay this kindness, and what better way than to try to help reestablish the precious dharma in the land of its origin, India. Lama Yeshe suggested creating a center for the study and practice of Buddhism. The name he decided upon was Tushita Mahayana Meditation Centre. Lama Yeshe already had a retreat center called Tushita in Dharamsala, the home of His Holiness and the Ti-

betan government in exile. Tushita is a Sanskrit
name for the pure land presided over by
Maitreya, the future Buddha, who will appear on
earth to reestablish the dharma once the era of
Guru Shākyamuni Buddha's teachings has passed.
In Tibetan, the word is *"Ganden,"* which was the
name of the first of many great monasteries established by Lama Tsong Khapa and his followers
in Tibet. It means "Land of Joy."

After a two-year search, in 1979, with the help
of one of his Indian students, Lama Yeshe found
an ideal house in the New Delhi suburb of Shantiniketan to serve as the center, which then began
to offer a daily routine of morning and evening
meditations and frequent teachings by some of
the great exiled Tibetan lamas such as His Holiness's own senior tutor, Kyabje Ling Rinpoche
(1903–83), his junior tutor, Kyabje Trijang Rinpoche (1901–81), Tsenshab Serkong Rinpoche
(1914–83), Song Rinpoche (1905–83), Geshe
Sopa Rinpoche and Geshe Rabten Rinpoche.
Lama Gelek Rinpoche, who at that time was
resident in New Delhi, also became a regular
teacher. Many Indian scholars and Western Buddhist practitioners also taught at Tushita, and several of these teachings were published by the
center in 1981 in a book entitled *Teachings at*

Tushita. The center also served as a guest house for Buddhist pilgrims from all over the world, and Lama Yeshe, too, enjoyed staying there whenever he passed through New Delhi. Of course, Lama Yeshe himself imparted many lesson there.

Since 1974, at the request of his many international students, Lama Yeshe, who was based at Kopan Monastery, Kathmandu, Nepal, had been traveling the world each year, preaching, initiating people and establishing dharma centers in many different countries such as the United States, Australia, New Zealand, England, Italy and France. In 1975, Lama Yeshe created an organization, the Foundation for the Preservation of the Mahayana Tradition (FPMT), in order to facilitate the development of this global dharma network and to make sure that only the pure teachings of the Buddha were taught at his centers. Tushita became a part of this network of teaching and retreat centers, monasteries, publishing houses and other related activities, which now number more than 110 in over twenty countries worldwide. Included in these dharma activities are numerous projects in Buddh Gaya, the site of Lord Buddha's Enlightenment: a leprosy project, a school and a home for the destitute and the building of a five-hundred-foot-high statue of Maitreya Buddha.

In 1981, Lama Yeshe requested His Holiness Tenzin Gyatso, the fourteenth Dalai Lama of Tibet, to teach at Tushita. The lineage of the Dalai Lamas goes back to the time of Lama Tsong Khapa, whose nephew and student, Gendun Drub (1391–1474), became the first Dalai Lama, although he was not recognized as such during his lifetime. It was the great fifth Dalai Lama, Gyalwa Ngawang Losang Gyatso (1617–82), who united Tibet under Gelugpa rule and built that enduring image of Tibet, the Potala Palace, the winter quarters of the Dalai Lamas and seat of the Tibetan government from the seventeenth century until 1959. His Holiness's predecessor, Gyalwa Thubten Gyatso (1876–1933), was known as the Great Thirteenth for his wise and perceptive leadership of Tibet during the profound global changes of the early part of this century.

The Dalai Lamas are recognized as incarnations of Avalokiteshvara, the Buddha of Compassion, and it is a great blessing even to be in their presence, let alone receive teachings from them. Therefore, Lama Yeshe thought it would be a wonderful thing for the people of New Delhi to have the chance to receive His Holiness's teachings. Accordingly, Lama Yeshe requested him to teach at an event sponsored by Tushita in the autumn of 1981, which Lama Yeshe called a "dharma celebration." His Holiness graciously accepted, and thus the tradition of Tushita dharma celebrations began with an event at New Delhi's Ashoka Hotel, which was attended by more than four hundred people, mostly residents of Delhi. Now each time His Holiness imparts his teachings at the dharma celebrations in New Delhi, the auditoriums or halls throng with over two thousand to three thousand people.

Tragically, in 1984 Lama Yeshe passed away. A year or so later, the lease on the Shantiniketan house expired and Tushita moved to an apartment in Nizamuddin East. Every couple of years thereafter, the center kept moving and it is now located in Padmini Enclave, Hauz Khas, New Delhi.

The *Lam-rim* teachings are the essence of Tibetan Buddhism, the heart of the Vajrayana, and constitute the core of the teachings we offer at Tushita. Their basis is the understanding that the mind, or each individual's stream of consciousness, has no beginning, and that since beginningless time, each sentient being's mind has been polluted by ignorance, attachment and aversion.

The influence of these negative thoughts causes us to create negative karma, the result of which is the experience of suffering, such as rebirth in unfortunate states, pain, illness and all the other misfortunes that befall us and others. However, although they have always been there, these negative thoughts are not a permanent part of the mind. Through proper means they can be completely eradicated, revealing the mind's basic clear light nature, and freeing a person from suffering forever.

What are these proper means? They include transforming one's mind through practice of the *Lam-rim* teachings. One way to understand this is to contemplate in the first person the key teachings of the path to Enlightenment in the form of a motivation, as follows:

Since beginningless time, in all my numberless previous lives, I have been dying and being reborn in samsara, the six suffering realms of cyclic existence. This time, at last, I have received a perfect human rebirth, which has eight freedoms and ten richnesses. This offers me an unparalleled opportunity to strive for meaningful goals, such as attaining Enlightenment for the sake of all sentient beings, liberation from the beginningless cycle of suffering or, at least, better future lives in samsara. If, instead, I again waste my time by attaching myself to the comforts of just this life, I will completely destroy this priceless opportunity.

This precious life was not easy to get. It has resulted from my practicing dharma in many previous lives, for example, keeping pure morality, practicing generosity and offering sincere prayers for the welfare of others. Thus, it will not be easy to receive again. Therefore, I must not waste this rare chance to benefit myself and others.

Furthermore, this life is extremely short. I am certain to die but I have no idea when death will come. My life is constantly running out, faster than I can imagine, without pausing for a moment. And when I die, nothing but the dharma I have practiced will help. All the things I have worked for—power, position and possessions—will only hinder my chances of rebirth into a better future life. Therefore, I must practice dharma and only dharma, right now.

If I do not practice dharma but simply continue to create negative karma and do not purify the vast amount I have already created in this and previous lives, I will be reborn in one of the lower realms—in hell, or the hungry ghost or animal realms—from which it is almost impossible to escape and where I will experience continuous, unbearable suffering. If I were to die right now, and what's to say that I won't, I would certainly find myself in one of these terrifying places.

Who can guide me in this time of utmost need? The three jewels—Buddha, dharma and sangha—are my only hope. Therefore, out of fear of the suffering of the three lower realms and with complete confidence in their ability to guide me, I must turn to the three jewels for refuge. How do they protect me? By showing me the path to freedom from suffering. But it is up to me to follow the path they show. The essence of this is observing the law of karma.

Karma is definite: good karma brings happiness; bad karma brings suffering. Therefore I must create only good karma and avoid bad karma at all costs. By practicing in this way I can at least be reborn in the upper realms.

But upper rebirth is not enough. As I know from my present experience as a human, even in the upper realms there is great suffering—illness, injury, aging and death; not getting what I want; losing what I have; meeting with disagreeable circumstances. Being anywhere in samsara itself is suffering, because I am always vulnerable to one sort of misery or another and never know what will strike or when. Therefore, I must liberate myself completely from the wheel of uncontrolled death and rebirth and thus attain the everlasting peace and happiness of nirvana.

But neither is this enough. Attachment to my own personal peace and striving solely for this is very selfish and cruel. All sentient beings want to find happiness and avoid suffering. In this, I am equal with all others. Furthermore, I am one and they are infinite in number; therefore, their happiness is much more important than my own. Also, all my past, present and future happiness— from the tiniest enjoyment, such as a cool breeze on a hot day, all the way up to the never-ending bliss of Enlightenment—depends upon other sentient beings. Not only that, but each and every sentient being has been my mother on countless occasions, exhibiting a mother's kindness to me every time. Therefore, for these and many other reasons, I must repay all this kindness in the highest possible way: by leading all sentient beings to the supreme Enlightenment of Buddhahood.

However, at the moment I can hardly keep myself out of suffering. It is difficult enough to lead others to ordinary happiness, let alone Enlightenment. Only an enlightened being can lead others to Buddhahood; therefore, in order to repay the kindness of others, I must first become enlightened myself. In order to do this I must find a fully qualified teacher and study, contemplate and meditate on the teachings of the Buddha. This is the most meaningful way of spending my life; therefore, this is what I shall do.

His Holiness the Dalai Lama is the perfect teacher, the great treasure of infinite compassion embracing all sentient beings, our sole source of benefit and happiness, our sole refuge. His Holiness is kinder than the three-time Buddhas. Therefore, if merely to hold this book of His Holiness's teachings in our hands is a great blessing, what more can be said of reading his words, contemplating their meaning and meditating upon them to realize their ultimate truth?

May this teaching benefit all sentient beings and create the cause for them to attain Enlightenment; especially, may this benefit all the Indian people. May anyone who sees, touches, remembers or thinks about this book never be reborn in the lower realms. May all the wrong views toward the doctrine immediately be pacified. May all Indian people have unshakable faith only in refuge and karma; may they all have strong

devotion to Buddhism and actualize the whole
path to Enlightenment, especially *bodhicitta,* in
this very lifetime. May they be inspired to spread
and learn dharma. But especially, may all the
wrong views be immediately pacified. May the
Indian people want to learn Buddhism and attain
Enlightenment, and may they practice to actualize the entire path.

My experience of people in India, especially in
Delhi, inspires me to think about how important
it is to really seriously question the quality of
one's own life, to examine one's inner life and to
check the state of one's mind. Are you really
happy with the way you live your life now? Is it
really satisfying and fulfilling? It is important that
you should guide yourself, that you should liberate yourself.

We can talk about all the philosophies of the
East and West, all the different religions and the
many things associated with them. The Bhagavad
Gita, Bible and Koran . . . we can read all the religious texts. We can talk and talk and talk of all
these philosophies all our lives and yet have nothing develop in our hearts. Our hearts remain
empty, we don't achieve any essence in this life.
We get worse and worse, our brains get filled
with words like the computer yet our real inner

life continues to be empty and meaningless. There is no spiritual development in our hearts and we do not renounce the three poisonous minds of ignorance, attachment and hatred. This creates all problems in our life, now and in the future, especially the problems caused by the ego-centered mind and self-cherishing thoughts that harm all sentient beings. Nothing is developed in the fundamental spiritual path of compassion and loving kindness to others. Our real inner life remains arid even though our brain is full of words.

What everyone, an uneducated person, a professor, philosopher, beggar or millionaire, a child, an old person, yourself or others, is looking for is happiness; nobody wants problems and suffering. Where happiness is concerned, you can focus either on the happiness of the moment, or on happiness that transcends lifetimes. There is happiness that lasts a minute, one hour, twelve hours or twenty-four hours; which happiness do you want? Which happiness do you think is most important to achieve? Similarly, there is happiness that can last for one week, a month, or years. So, which one would you prefer? Which one is most important?

At present, it seems as though one's life span is long. We carry the concept of permanence in our hallucinated minds and important phenomena, such as life, are mistakenly apprehended as being permanent. We believe that we are going to live for a long time. This happens naturally. The day when death comes, this life is gone, the appearance is gone; life happened and is now gone. It feels as though your human life was as brief as lightning. If lightning strikes when you are outside in dark weather, with no moon and in completely foggy surroundings, the lightning illuminates your body and the things around you vividly. There is the sudden appearance one moment, and the next minute it is gone.

Death is just like this for ordinary beings who haven't reached the level on the path where you can be free from the suffering of the cycle of death and rebirth. Until you reach that level, death is a certainty and can happen at any time, and at any moment. Therefore, we must consider the happiness of future lives that is more important than the happiness of just this one life. Until you are free from the cycle of death and rebirth, you will continue to have many lives. How long it will take to be free from this cycle depends on whether you can actualize the unmistaken, reliable and proven path. Even if this path is not proven by you, it has been proven by others who examined, experimented and actualized their freedom from the cycle of death and rebirth. So, since your wish is for happiness, you have to make all those imminent future lives happy, not meaningless and full of suffering. And then, even more important than the happiness of future lives is the everlasting happiness, the cessation of suffering.

For the human being, there is the suffering of rebirth, old age, sickness as well as death; there are also problems that arise from undesirable objects, in addition to worries from desirable objects and the inability to find desirable objects. Even when one has finally found what one desires, one is unable to find satisfaction from this object. This is what disturbs people and gives rise to many problems in the world. Fruit may look beautiful on the outside, but on the inside be totally rotten with worms—in the same way, our life may be externally nice looking, everything might look fine, while internally it may be hell. Many times when you come to know a person you desire, when you come close to the person, in a few days, after a few hours, maybe even just minutes, what you find is that externally the person is attractive but inside he or she is not so nice.

All these sufferings are painful, but this is not the only suffering of samsara. There is the second type of suffering—temporary pleasure—that is actually suffering. Why? Because this feeling seems pleasurable to our hallucinated mind, but when we analyze the feeling with wisdom, we realize that it is only suffering. Temporary samsaric pleasures include having a good reputation, receiving praise, the sensual pleasures of man and woman, food, drinking, smoking, eating, sleeping, receiving gifts, wealth and so forth.

Then there is the third type of suffering, which is the most important one to realize. This arises from the five aggregates of our contaminated body/mind that are in the nature of suffering, the seed of the contaminated aggregates produced by delusion and karma. Our body/mind is the product of an impure cause. It stems from the contaminated seeds of disturbing thoughts and this is why it is in the nature of suffering. A disturbing thought can only produce another disturbing thought. The mind fills with depression and loneliness; the mind always feels dissatisfied, empty, fearful because there is so much expectation and clinging to this and that. There are so many worries, the inability to obtain what you want and fears that you will not get what you want. Then, especially, there is the suffering that comes when you don't get what you want. Also, there are all the physical problems, the various sicknesses that are unbearable. There are all the problems of old age, all the difficulties of being so fragile, so delicate.

So the big question to examine is, Why not experience great bliss instead of pain? For this, one has to first find out who has been able to do it. By knowing who created the cause of bliss instead of suffering, you can learn the solution. Then you can come to know what liberation to achieve.

Then you come to the unmistaken path, the method that really ends the cause of suffering, and through that path you stop the production of suffering. This includes ending the suffering arising from the continuation of the contaminated aggregates that circle from life to life. This cessation of pervasive compounding suffering is the real liberation. If you don't experience either of the two other types of suffering (painful experience and short-lived pleasure) you can't be liberated. These can cease only temporarily until you end samsara completely through the cessation of the continuation of the contaminated aggregates.

This cessation guards you from the suffering of hell, hungry ghosts and animals. You are freed from their suffering forever. A greater happiness is the cessation of even the subtle negative imprint that is left by the concept of inherent existence—the inherent existence of "I," or the self. You attain the totally pure, perfect state of mind, the state of full Enlightenment, peerless happiness, complete bliss; there is nothing more to gain. This achievement is the most important one because it benefits all sentient beings by liberating them from suffering and leading them to Enlightenment. With all this in mind, you have to decide how you want to lead your life.

Enlightenment—the total cessation of suffering and the ability to lead all beings to that state—is the most important reason why you should not waste the life that can bring the most benefit not only to you, but to all sentient beings. To begin the process of Enlightenment, we must investigate the nature of our mind. Our mind is like the reflection in a clean mirror. The mind, like the mirror, has no obstruction of form. Objects appear and the mind perceives them, yet the mind itself is shapeless and colorless. It does not cease to exist at the time of death even when it loses the vehicle, the body. It is everlasting. To understand reincarnation, one needs to have an understanding of the mind.

The mind didn't come into existence independently, without causes and conditions. All delusions—pride, jealousy, ignorance, and so forth—are forever changing due to causes and conditions. Since the mind is a causative phenomenon, it is impermanent. It exists under the control of causes and conditions. It changes due to causes and conditions. For example, anger rises due to causes and conditions. There is, in addition, the imprint left on the mind by anger from the past. When a person doesn't control the mind, or protect it with a remedy of meditation or psychology, anger rises because of the imprints left by past anger and the external condition of encountering undesirable objects. The mind is responsible for how one encounters the undesirable object; it is the mind that gives a negative interpretation to an object, with negative reasoning. We believe in these reasons and attach an unpleasant label to the object; anger arises. Thus, our mind creates the object of anger as well. Therefore your enemy and what you retaliate against are actually products of your own mind.

The main cause for anger is the negative imprint from past anger that resides in your mental consciousness. Anger arises if you do not have any patience for the object or enemy. It's just a different way of thinking about a person, unlike a person who is attached to you and likes you. Patience is what makes you label a negative experience positively. Patience generates a positive, peaceful and healthy mind.

A dissatisfied person full of hatred or anger becomes positive if he or she generates patience. Patience offers you the greatest advantage and benefit in life, the best spiritual development. It transforms your mind, teaches you to be even more patient and abates anger. You cease to have enemies in this life and all future lives.

The goal in life is not to harm others, but to benefit others, make their life useful, free them from problems, develop compassion and wisdom to create greater happiness for others. By understanding suffering and our mind, we can find the motivation to attain these goals and fulfill the purpose of life. The most important activity is to live the twenty-four hours of the day with this attitude. Compassion and wisdom fill the empty heart with joy.

Lama Thubten Zopa Rinpoche

Transforming
Mind

In order to practice Buddhism, you have to first know about the mind. Even if you are a nonbeliever you can try to improve or train the mind, provided you have knowledge of it. Any normal human being, for that matter, can practice training the mind and this will eventually prove to be very useful.

Essentially, this is what the Eight Verses are about. They teach us how to deal with our negative emotions and subsequently improve or transform our mind. As a practitioner, you must pay heed to your mind to constantly try and control it. You should try to eliminate all negative emotions and develop positive ones—infinitely—particularly in the practice of Buddhism, since some people say that Buddhism is the science of the mind.

Everyone wants happiness; nobody wants to suffer. Many problems around us are a mental projection of certain negative or unpleasant things. If we analyze our own mental attitude, we may find it quite unbearable. Therefore, a well-balanced mind is very useful and we should try and have a stable mental state.

Everybody wants a healthy body and nobody wants to be sick. I, for one, don't like falling ill but very often I get a cold—especially when I visit Buddh Gaya. Almost every time I am there, the blessing is so great that I always get flu! But the fact remains that everybody wants good health, and one of the important means for attaining it is a stable mind.

Mental training is crucial for good health. Good health and stability of the mind signify a good and happier life and a sound future. Although a person may be in a hostile environment, if one's mental attitude is firm and stable, the hostility will not be a cause for much disturbance. Without inner mental stability, or the right mental attitude, one cannot be happy, calm or at peace, even if one is surrounded by the best of friends or the best facilities. This is why training the mind is imperative and should not be considered a religious matter. Some technique or method for training the mind should be a part of everyone's daily life. The mind is colorless, formless and difficult to identify. Yet, it is powerful. Sometimes it seems difficult to check, change and control. I think much depends on time, will, determination and wisdom. If we have determination and wisdom—wisdom implying knowledge—the point, then, is how to train the mind. Eventually, with the passage of time, our mind can change and improve. For example, of my parents, my mother was extraordinarily gentle and had a lot of patience, whereas my father was very short-tempered. In the early part of my life, I was much closer to my father, and thus more prone to anger. During the latter part of my life I was closer to my mother and therefore much calmer. I learned from both of them. Traditionally, Tibetans believe that the people who come from the Amdo area are more short-tempered and straightforward. Since I belong to that area, I have a good excuse for my anger!

You can train your mind by analyzing the shortcomings of anger as well as from other people's experiences. It is also useful to look at history. Whenever I examine human tragedy, I find that in most cases it is the result of human behavior— negative emotions such as anger, hatred, jealousy and extreme greed. All good things that are constructive, happier human experiences, are mostly

motivated by respect for others' rights and concern for others' well-being—compassion, love
and kindness.

A very thorough investigation of past human
experiences and events, and one's daily practice,
is imperative to bring about change and improve-
ment. We human beings are similar in our desires. This is why training the mind is important.

The Eight Verses explain the importance of altruism, and how to preserve it when we come across
difficult situations in our daily life. For human beings as well as animals, the foundation of society
is affection or love. During the period when we
are in our mothers' wombs, the mother's mental
stability and calmness are very important for the
development of the unborn child. Also, the first
few weeks after birth are a crucial period for development of the brain. During that period it is
extremely important to have the mother's physical touch. This shows that the physical condition
itself needs the warmth and affection of others.
The human baby's first act after birth is sucking
milk. Giving or receiving milk certainly does not
stem from hatred or negative feelings. Although
at that time the baby's mind is not clear and does
not have a clear idea of its mother, a bond or feel-

ing of closeness is definitely established. However, if the mother's mind has anger or some negative feelings toward the child, the milk may not flow. It is deep affection and a feeling of intimacy toward the baby that allows the milk to flow properly. And turning to the mother for milk is our first act as human beings.

Over the next few months and years we are heavily dependent on others, mainly our parents or guardians. Without their kindness and responsibility, the child cannot survive. As students, we find that if a teacher is affectionate or close to us, then the lessons as well as the teacher leave a lasting impression on us.

From time to time we need to visit doctors even if we don't want to. Although the doctor may be highly qualified, if the doctor's face is stiff and bereft of a smile, we feel slightly uncomfortable. If the doctor shows genuine concern about our health and is affectionate, we feel comfortable.

When we get older, we depend heavily once again on the affection and kindness of others. This is human nature. Since human beings are social creatures, we depend heavily on one another in order to survive.

Even small animals and insects like bees and

ants possess some kind of social instinct. They have a great sense of responsibility and work together in tandem. If we look at bees, we find that they work on the basis of cooperation even though they have no religion, constitution or laws. Their natural form and way of life demand that they work together; otherwise, they cannot survive. Humans claim to be superior beings but we are, in fact, sometimes inferior to these small insects. Our basic situation demands that we live together, and, hence, we work together. It is a natural law but sometimes we act in quite the contrary manner.

According to Buddhism, plants have no mind or consciousness. As a Buddhist monk, I say they have no consciousness, but I don't know, it's difficult to tell. I think we need to investigate further. Some people say that plants have some kind of feeling or cognitive power. Even without consciousness or mind, their very existence is based on the cooperation of each particle and cell. Each particle has a special duty or role and all the particles work together to allow the plant to survive and develop. Similarly, the function and existence of the world, the planet itself, even the universe, depend on cooperation.

Different parts of the human body work together, allowing us to function effectively. Our existence and survival depend on the cooperation and coordination of these parts. Take, for instance, the human family. In the absence of cooperation and understanding, parents and children are always fighting. The same is true of quarrels between couples. Divorce ensues and no peace or happiness remains. The marriage is ruined. Cooperation is imperative for a healthy family, body, society and nation. How does one develop cooperation? By force? Impossible! So what is the alternative? Voluntary actions, altruism and showing concern for the welfare and rights of others. These need not be considered sacred; they are in one's own interest because one's survival depends on it. For example, if you are concerned about other people and genuinely friendly toward them, then other people will also respond appropriately.

I love smiles and laughter. If one wants more smiles in one's life, one must create the right conditions for it. There are many different kinds of smiles. Some smiles that are diplomatic or sarcastic create an unpleasant atmosphere and give rise to suspicion, whereas a genuine smile gives us a great deal of satisfaction. So how does one achieve that? Certainly not through anger, jealousy, extreme greed or hatred, but through loving kindness, an open mind and sincerity.

If your motives are sincere, there is nothing to hide, and you get an open attitude in return. This is the real and proper channel of human communication and not mere lip service. From my own experience, sometimes I find I can communicate sincerely even when I don't know the other person's language. But at times it is difficult to be candid.

When people have power, others tend to flock around them. I think I have more friends now because of the Nobel Peace Prize. These friends may not be very reliable. People with fame, power or wealth usually have many friends. These friends, in fact, may not be true friends; they are attracted only to the wealth or power of the person concerned. If the person loses his power or wealth, these friends may disappear. I consider such friends insincere.

True friends share genuine closeness and remain friends irrespective of fluctuating fortunes. Such concern for others is a great virtue but it is also selfish in a way since it's ultimately for one's own benefit and interest. Very often I tell my friends that if we have to be selfish, we should be wisely selfish. If we are sincere we will have reliable friends and benefit greatly. If you neglect others, forget about their welfare and think only about yourself, eventually you'll be the loser.

Thus, the basic structure of human society requires a sense of responsibility based on altruism and compassion. The ultimate source of happiness is altruism. Success in life depends on determination, will and courage. And the source of this courage and determination is altruism. Sometimes anger and hatred create a kind of energy and determination. This determination, however, rarely has good consequences because the energy created by anger and jealousy is blind, harmful and can even be fatal.

The Buddhist technique or method to improve the mind is based on the theory of interdependence, or *pratityasamutpada*. This is mainly concerned with the causes of pain and pleasure and the fact that everything is interlinked, creating a chain reaction. As I mentioned earlier, satisfaction or happiness depends on a variety of factors. Therefore, *pratityasamutpada* actually widens our worldview. It shows us that everything is ultimately related to our benefit. Naturally, this enables us to develop concern for the wider perspective. Understanding this theory and actually putting it to practice can promote loving kindness and compassion, and reduce one's anger and hatred.

According to Buddhism, there is a commensurate relationship between cause and effect where pain and pleasure are concerned. The immediate cause is karma. Karma means action. Tomorrow's events depend very much on today's actions, this year's events on last year's, while this century's events are linked with those of the previous centuries. The actions of previous generations affect the lives of the generations that follow. This is also a kind of karma. However, there is a difference between actions carried out by a group of people or sentient beings jointly, and actions carried out by a single person. In individual cases, the actions of the earlier part of one's life have an effect on the latter part of one's life.

What, then, is the source of action? What is the motivation of mind? And, more important, what is mind? Is it the brain or a kind of energy produced by the brain? The answer is both. It is both because while the grosser level of consciousness is produced by the brain, the ultimate source of consciousness is the innermost subtle consciousness that is not dependent on the brain. So what is the cause of ultimate and innermost subtle consciousness? There are two causes: a "substantial" cause and a "cooperative" cause.

Human beings took five billion years to develop to their present human state. For three to four billion years there was no life, only some basic, primary cells. In spite of human evolution, the question still remains, Why did the whole universe or galaxy come into existence at all? What is the reason? We could say that there is no reason or that it suddenly happened, but that answer is not satisfactory.

Another answer is that it was the creator's, or God's, doing. However, this view does not hold true for Buddhist and Jain philosophies. The Buddhist answer is that it came into existence as a result of the karma of the beings who would utilize these galaxies. Take the example of a house. A house exists because there is a builder who constructs it so that it can be used. Similarly, because there were sentient beings to inhabit or utilize this galaxy, their karma produced the galaxy.

We cannot explain this on a physical basis, only on the basis of the continuation of mind. The most subtle consciousness or mind has no beginning and no end. That is its ultimate nature. I am not talking about absolute nature here. Even on the conventional level, ultimate nature is something that is pure. The grosser mind with its basis of consciousness has its own ultimate nature that is pure. It can be influenced by negative emotions as well as by positive thought. All negative emotions are based on ignorance and ignorance has no solid basis.

According to Buddhist philosophy, every sentient being who has a mind and consciousness has the potential to become a Buddha. This subtle consciousness is termed *Buddhaseed* or *sugatahridaya,* or tathagatagarbha. This is the basis of Buddhism in general and Mahayana Buddhism in particular. In Mahayana Buddhism, the ultimate goal is Buddhahood or Enlightenment. One should be determined to achieve Buddhahood in order to serve all sentient beings. This determination is *bodhicitta,* which is the basis of the Mahayana teaching of infinite altruism.

To develop *bodhicitta* we have to first know about the Four Noble Truths. It is possible to end suffering or bring about cessation. In order to do that, we have to know what suffering is and what causes it. Only then can cessation be achieved and the true path followed. It will help us if we develop determination and altruism. We should recite the Eight Verses every day, making them a part of our daily life. When we are faced with problems, we should immediately read, recite and practice the Eight Verses. This is difficult to implement but it is better to make an attempt so that we have no regrets later.

I

With the determination to accomplish
The highest welfare for all sentient beings,
Who excel even the wish-granting gem,
May I at all times hold them dear.

This verse proclaims that in order to achieve Buddhahood we must develop infinite altruism and create good actions. We depend heavily on other sentient beings. Without sentient beings we cannot develop infinite altruism and cannot achieve Buddhahood. We owe our fame, wealth and friends to other sentient beings. For example, without other sentient beings one cannot have woolen clothes, since one cannot have wool without sheep. The media is responsible for fame and so on; even reputations are dependent entirely on other sentient beings.

From conception till death, our life depends on others. It is important to realize how other sentient beings are precious and useful. As soon as we realize this, our negative attitude toward other beings will change.

II

Whenever I associate with someone,
May I think myself the lowest among all
And hold the other supreme
In the depth of my heart.

Our attitude toward other people should always be positive. We should be concerned about others without feeling pity for them. Above all, we should treat them with great respect for they are precious. We should consider them as sacred and superior to ourselves.

III

In all actions may I search my mind,
And as soon as klesha, or delusion, arises,
Endangering myself and others,
May I firmly face and avert it.

IV

When I see beings of wicked nature,
Pressed by violent sin and affliction,
May I hold these rare ones dear,
As if I had found a precious treasure.

These verses explain how to control one's negative emotions. Our mind is greatly influenced by negative emotions due to our infinite past lives and it is extremely difficult to develop altruism. We have to fight constantly against these negative emotions. We have to use different methods to deal with the forces of anger. It is difficult to control sudden, intense anger. You should simply try to forget about the object of anger and divert your attention. Concentrate on your breathing. This cools down the anger slightly. Then try to think about the negative aspects of anger and minimize or get rid of it.

There is another type of anger that is not very forceful. One way to deal with the anger toward one's enemy is to focus on the enemy's good qualities. Try to develop respect and sympathy instead. As in *pratityasamutpada,* every object has many aspects and faces. Almost no object can be wholly negative. Everything has a positive side to it. When anger develops, however, our mind perceives only the negative aspect.

On the one hand, our enemy creates problems for us. On the other, that very person gives us the opportunity to practice patience and tolerance, two qualities necessary for compassion and altruism.

When extreme greed or other negative emotions arise, one should be prepared for them. If you take a lenient attitude when the negative emotion arises, it becomes stronger. So reject or try to reduce it right from its inception.

V

When others out of envy treat me badly
With abuse, slander and the like,
May I suffer the defeat
And offer the victory to others.

VI

If someone whom I have benefited
With great hope hurts me very badly,
May I behold him
As my supreme guru.

This is difficult to practice but essential if we want to develop genuine altruism. Some *bodhisattva* practices seem impossible and unrealistic; nonetheless, they are important.

If we are humble and honest, a certain someone might take advantage of us. Even in such situations, we should not harbor any negative feelings toward that person. Instead, we should analyze the situation. Allowing that person to do whatever he or she likes will ultimately be harmful for that person. Therefore, we should take some countermeasures. We should do this not because that person has harmed us, but because we should be concerned about the person's well-being in the long run.

When anger dominates our mind, the best part of the human brain, which judges situations, fails in its function. We may then use harsh words unintentionally. Hateful words pour out automatically due to lack of control when we cannot handle a situation. Once the anger subsides, we feel ashamed of ourselves.

VII

May I directly and indirectly
Offer benefit and happiness to all my mothers;
May I secretly take upon myself
The harm and suffering of the mothers.

This verse tells us to benefit other sentient beings more than oneself and take on their suffering. This can be practiced through deep breathing— taking in suffering and breathing out happiness. One can also do this by visualizing or training the mind through focusing on the object of meditation.

VIII

May all this remain undefiled by the stains,
Keeping in view the eight worldly principles,
May I, by perceiving all dharmas as illusive,
Unattached, be delivered from bondage, samsara.

In order to meditate on ultimate altruism, it's important to understand the concept. In Buddhism, various levels of tenets have different interpretations of it. Of the four philosophical schools, the interpretation given here is referred to in the highest Buddhist tenets, *Prasangika-Madhyamika*. According to this, emptiness means that no phenomenon can have an inherent existence. By understanding the lack of inherent existence of all nature, we can understand the illusive nature or the illusion of all phenomena.

Practice infinite altruism with the help of wisdom. That's the way.

Constitution Club Lawns, 1990

A Journey to

Happiness

As human beings we are basically all the same; after all we all belong to the same planet. All sentient beings have the same innate nature that wants happiness and doesn't want to suffer. All of us love ourselves and desire something good. Now, as far as material development is concerned, we have already achieved a great deal, and every nation on this planet is aiming for better facilities and is attempting to create a more prosperous society.

Eventually we may achieve that. However, material development alone is not sufficient for human happiness. The reason is quite simple: human beings are not the product of a machine; we are something more. Therefore, we need more than just external objects in order to be happy.

The most important thing in life is human affection. Without it one cannot achieve genuine happiness. And if we want a happier life, a happier

family, happier neighbors or a happier nation, the
key is inner quality. Even if the five billion human
beings that inhabit the earth become million-
aires, without inner development there cannot
be peace or any lasting happiness. Some people
may be very rich, but we often find that they are
not happy at all. Affection, love and compassion
are some of the most important elements in our
life. Peace of mind is crucial for good health. Of
course good facilities, the right medicine and
food also make a difference. But happiness is the
most important factor for good health.

Everybody is concerned about world peace.
Weapons or military force, under certain circumstances at certain times, can produce some
relative peace. In the long run, however, it is impossible to achieve genuine and lasting world
peace through military confrontation, or hatred
and suspicion. World peace must develop
through mental peace, mutual trust and mutual
respect. For that, again, compassion or altruistic
mind is the key factor.

Let us consider the significance of a happy family. The most important thing is affection.
Whether we are successful in life or not depends
a lot on the atmosphere we grow up in. Children
from families full of love and compassion are hap-

pier and more successful human beings. On the other hand, a child's life may be ruined if he or she grows up in fear or lacks love and affection.

Where does affection come from and how can one develop or increase human affection? So long as the human mind exists, the seed of affection exists. Although negative and positive thoughts and emotions are all part of the human mind, the dominant force in human consciousness or human life is affection. Therefore, the seed of compassion is a part of one's nature right from birth. When we are born, we are free from all ideology and religion that come later, but we are not free from the need for human affection. A baby cannot survive without it.

Affection is an important element in conception. Human affection and compassion are not just about love or seeking pleasure. True compassion is not only about sympathy or a feeling of closeness, but a sense of responsibility as well. Genuine compassion is generated when we realize that people who suffer or lack happiness or prosperity want happiness just like us. Compassion is about developing genuine concern for them.

Usually we think of compassion as a feeling of closeness toward our friends but that is a view tainted by mental projections. As long as a person is a close friend, we have a positive attitude toward him or her. As soon as that person's attitude changes or as soon as our feelings toward that person change, compassion ceases to exist as well. This is not really compassion, but more of an attachment.

Genuine compassion involves analyzing the situation regardless of whether the person is close or not. The fact remains that the person has a problem and is suffering, and has the same right as I do to overcome the suffering and to be happy.

Marriage and conception are not results of mad love alone. They come of knowing each other well. When you know your partner's mental attitude as well as his or her physical aspect, you can develop mutual trust and respect. It is only on that basis that marriage can take place. There is a sense of responsibility involved. Human conception should take place under such circumstances.

As human beings, we have intelligence and extraordinary abilities. Those who have more intelligence are more farsighted, and those who are more able also have a greater responsibility toward themselves as well as others. In fact, human beings are responsible not only for other human beings but for the well-being of other sentient beings and our planet as well. If we utilize our intelligence and abilities in a destructive manner, it will result in disaster and tragedy. We must utilize them constructively instead. I am quite sure that those with extraordinary intelligence and ability who manipulate other people or things for their own benefit end up having some deep regret.

I think that both humans and animals have an innate appreciation for truth. If we treat dogs or cats sincerely, they appreciate it. If we cheat them, they realize that, and don't like it. If one human being communicates truthfully with another, it is appreciated. If we cheat others, they will react accordingly, whether they are believers or nonbelievers, rich or poor, educated or uneducated. Therefore, compassion and honesty exist because we don't want to cheat people, and because we all have the same right to be happy. Compassion, as I mentioned earlier, is a combination of sympathy and concern, a feeling of closeness with a sense of responsibility.

Some people feel that compassion, love and forgiveness are religious matters. This is wrong. Love and compassion are imperative. There is no way we can ignore these things, whether one is a believer or not. They are necessary if we want happiness and if we want to be good citizens. As far as religion is concerned, if accepting a particular religion makes you comfortable, then you should take up that religion. If you do not want to, it doesn't matter; leave it. But it is important to understand the nature of compassion, because it is a basic and necessary human quality.

Happiness is mental. Machines cannot provide us with it, nor can we buy it. Money and wealth are only partial sources of happiness, not happiness per se. These will not produce happiness directly. Happiness must develop within ourselves; nobody can give it to us. Its ultimate source is tranquillity or peace of mind. It doesn't depend on external factors. It doesn't matter if we lack good facilities, a good education or a successful life, as long as we have inner confidence.

Concern and regard for others, and human affection, are extremely important factors for our happiness. Compassion gives us inner strength, a feeling of inner value.

Try to become a good human being with a warm heart, regardless of whether you are a politician, a religious person, a businessman or whatever. One's individual behavior can contribute to the making of a happier family and community.

Different religions come into being at different times and places. I feel that the various religions simply strengthen good human qualities; they minimize negative qualities while maximizing the good ones. All major world religions have the same message as far as love and compassion are concerned, although their expressions may be different. All religions realize the importance of love and forgiveness and have the potential to create and increase good human qualities.

Through the centuries, millions of people have benefited immensely from various religions. It is very unfortunate that different religious identities cause quarrels, turmoil and disunity. If we study the different religions and observe their potential to produce good human beings, there is enough reason to develop genuine respect for all religions.

There are two categories of religions. One group of religions I call theistic religions, such as Christianity, Islam, Judaism and Hinduism. These uphold a fundamental belief in God. Another group of religions I call godless religions, such as Buddhism, Jainism and Sankhya philosophy (an ancient and sophisticated component of Hinduism), believe there is no god, no creator and no almighty. Ultimately, the creator is one's own self. One group, mainly the Buddhists, does not accept the theory of a permanent soul. This demarcates Buddhism from non-Buddhism. The fundamental Buddhist theory is that there is no permanent soul or self. Within Buddhism, there are two distinctive groups on the basis of motivation: the Hinayana and the Mahayana. The motivation of the former is concerned mainly with one's own moksha, or salvation, through the practice of moral conduct and the convergence of mind and wisdom. The motivation of the other is not to think only of oneself, but to have concern for all living beings and pursue the practices of the six or ten paramitas, or perfections, to ultimately achieve Buddhahood. This is bodhisattvayana.

On the basis of philosophical tenets there are four different schools of thought: the Vaibhasikà, Sautrantika, Cittamatra and Madhyamika. The essence of Buddhist conduct according to all these schools is ahimsa, or nonviolence. Why is nonviolence so important? Because of the law of interdependence: that all things are interrelated. For example, survival depends on many factors as does one's happiness. Similarly, pain and tragedy depend on many factors. Just as we are concerned with our own happiness and experiences, we should also be concerned with their causes.

So the essence of Buddhist conduct and philosophy is nonviolence and the theory of interdependence, respectively. Nonviolence here has two directives: if you can, help and serve other sentient beings; if you cannot, then at least do not harm others.

The theory of interdependence is interpreted differently according to the various tenets. According to one, the meaning of interdependence is that all conditioned phenomena depend on causes. This implies that there is no creator; things depend only on their own causes and those causes in turn have their own causes, with no beginning. Everything changes because of these causes and conditions. New circumstances produce new events; these in turn act as causes and produce something different and new. This is the process of dependent arising: *pratityasamutpada*.

The concept of interdependence is accepted by all schools of Buddhist tenets. The interdependence theory expounded by the Madhyamika philosophy touches a slightly higher level in which interdependence involves everything being dependent on its parts. For example, if it is a physical object, it has different parts in the sense of having different directions. If it is formless, like consciousness, the meaning of having parts can be understood in terms of different levels of continuity or a stream. Similarly, space can be considered to be of interdependent origination because we can refer to space as having parts and we can think about a particular space with reference to specific objects and directions.

Interdependent origination is thus expounded not only in terms of dependence on causes and conditions, but also in terms of dependence on parts and directions.

A subtler level of interdependence is expounded by using the phrase "arising of things through designation or imputation." When we investigate, for example, what a flower actually is, and closely examine its particles, the flower ceases to be the flower we know. Further investigation of the smallest particles helps us understand that when we label something that designation is given because of the convergence of certain particles or substances. These particles come together to function as an entity and we give it a specific name. If we investigate "Who am I?" we fail to find an "I" apart from this body, brain or experience. If one goes deeper into the ultimate nature of oneself, one cannot find an independent and ultimate identity. We conventionally label the combination of body and mind and say, "This is a human being." This Tibetan flesh and mind from Amdo we label "Dalai Lama Tenzin Gyatso." After much analysis, however, if we really want to look for the Dalai Lama, we cannot find him.

Similarly, we use terms like "past," "present" and "future" all the time. In a way the past is mere memory, the future is just our thought, a plan or an idea. The present is real. If we think of the present eon, the present century, then in 1992, today, February 15, is the third week. Then the day, the hour, the minute, the second, a part of that second cease to be the "present." Just this moment. The past is gone. After this, the future is yet to come. There is no "present." Without a present we cannot identify "past" and "future." Time goes on without a stop, just keeps on going. This results in confusion.

This is as far as external time is concerned. In our internal experience, again I think that there's no past and no future—only the present. But if there is no past or future, there can be no present since the present depends entirely on the past, and the future depends entirely on the present. This is a natural law. There is no time otherwise.

When we say "time," of course time exists, but not without a basis of imputation or reference upon which we can label it; we cannot have an abstract sense of time. If we investigate, we do not really find anything. Ultimately we find something that is "empty."

However, this emptiness is not mere nothingness. Since all things are interdependent, independent identities or entities don't exist. When we investigate the ultimate nature of everything, we find it is the absence of independent existence. This is what we mean by "empty." Now, the absence of independent existence itself depends on other factors.

I am here and this is not a dream. This is not an illusion. It is real. If I pinch myself I feel pain because I have a body. I have a forefinger and thumb and they function. So there is something after all and yet we cannot find it in the ultimate analysis. In other words, emptiness and interdependent nature are two sides of the same coin.

The Buddha first taught the Four Noble Truths: true suffering, true origin of suffering, true cessation and true path on this basis. He taught them because suffering has causes and conditions and we do not want to suffer. He spoke about the origin of suffering. The Buddha taught us to identify suffering as well as its causes at different levels.

Our goal is happiness, which again depends on its own causes. Happiness can be temporary or permanent. Permanent happiness is more important, which is why the Buddha taught the third Noble Truth—that of true cessation; the cessation of suffering is the attainment of nirvana, or state of blissful happiness. He also spoke about the means by which one can actualize the state of cessation of suffering. That is the true path.

The Four Noble Truths consist of an explanation of happiness and suffering and their causes. The purpose of our life is happiness. From birth we have the right to be happy, and lasting happiness must develop within ourselves; nobody can give it to us and no external factor can be responsible for it. It must be achieved through our own inner development. How do we integrate the Four Noble Truths into our daily practice? First, it is important to know what mind is. People sometimes get the impression that the mind is an independent entity, separate from the body. Such a mind does not exist. We cannot find an independent "I" outside our body. Buddhists do not accept an independent "I," a permanent soul or self. However, since the mind depends on this body, we quite rightly refer to it as the human mind. If the mind were independent and had nothing to do with the body, there would be no distinction between animal and human minds.

As soon as the human brain ceases to function, the human mind ceases to exist. If that is so, then what is the theory of rebirth? The mind develops on the basis of causes and conditions both immediate and distant, direct and indirect.

For example, the mind that perceives a flower depends upon many conditions. One is the eye. Without this organ, even though we might have consciousness of the flower, or the flower before us, we will be unable to perceive the flower. On the other hand, the mind and eye alone without the flower could not develop an awareness of the flower. And if there was a flower, and a perfect eye but no brain, again we would not be aware of the flower.

The consciousness or mind is just a subtle energy upon which everything can be reflected. Its own nature is merely luminous. The Tibetan word *"shepa"* means "to be conscious of something." So besides the human brain, there are conditions, deeper and more subtle causes of human consciousness, without which the human mind cannot develop. We call that the clear light, the innermost subtle mind.

An indication of this is that at this moment while we utilize our sense organs fully, their level is very gross. But when we dream, certain organs are not active or their functions are reduced, and the mental state is deeper. And in the state of deep sleep without dreams, our mind attains its deepest level.

Another indication is when doctors declare someone dead and we find that the body remains without decaying for a few days, and in some cases, a few weeks. Because the innermost subtle mind is still present in the body, it continues to function. Therefore, in a deeper sense, that being has not yet departed from the body. The owner of the body, a controlling power, is still present, which is why the body does not decay. But medically or conventionally, that body is considered dead.

As far as I know, there have been at least ten or fifteen such incidents in India over the last thirty years. In my senior tutor's case, after he was declared clinically dead, he remained in the state of clear light for about thirteen days. Because of that we believe that there can be deep memory about past lives. Under certain conditions you can reflect on past experiences on the basis of clear light. Some practitioners go very deep when they meditate, and the grosser consciousness or grosser level of mind becomes inactive. Then they have memories of past lives of a hundred years ago, or in some cases events of several hundred years ago are somehow reflected in their mind.

Our explanation is that the innermost subtle mind is always present. Although momentarily changing, its continuity is permanent. So there are two levels of mind; the grosser level of mind depends entirely on this body but the most subtle mind is everlasting. On this basis rebirth takes place.

The mind's own basic nature is ultimately neutral. It can be influenced by negative as well as by positive emotions. Take, for instance, those who have a short temper. When I was young I was quite short-tempered. However, the mood never lasted for twenty-four hours. If negative emotions are in the very nature of our mind, then as long as the mind is functioning the anger must remain. That, however, is not the case. Similarly, positive emotions are also not in the nature of the mind. The mind is something neutral, reflecting all sorts of different experiences or phenomena.

Furthermore, what is the demarcation between negative and positive emotions? There is no absolute demarcation but a relative one. Those emotions, such as compassion, love and wisdom that produce a happiness more subtle, permanent, lasting and satisfactory, are positive. That is because we consider happiness as something good and something we must achieve. Everything that can help in that direction we consider positive. These positive emotions ultimately transform us into happier persons, more reliable and trustworthy. That is so because they are good although we cannot identify them as such in the absolute sense. Everybody appreciates them on the conventional level and therefore these are positive emotions.

Although positive and negative emotions are both equally powerful, the negative emotions usually occur without much reason and are really just an emotion. If we objectively examine the value of anger, hatred, jealousy, doubt, suspicion or fear, we see that there is no profound basis for such emotions. On the other hand, love, compassion and forgiveness have more profound bases or reasons. From a Buddhist viewpoint, especially the viewpoint of Madhyamika philosophy, these negative emotions are ultimately based on ignorance.

Ignorance here refers to a consciousness that perceives the nature of objects as having an independent existence. It is quite clear that when certain negative emotions develop, at that moment the object we feel negatively toward appears as absolute, something 100 percent negative. As long as that emotion exists, that object is absolutely negative. As soon as that emotion reduces, the overall impression also becomes more positive. This shows how negative emotions cannot function without the help of ignorance.

All negative emotions, therefore, are based on such ignorance. This ignorance or misconception, no matter how powerful, can be eliminated. Through investigation and meditation we can develop deeper understanding. Subsequently, the negativity will be reduced and ultimately eliminated. That is the nature of mind.

We all have an innate desire for happiness. Happiness and unhappiness depend on positive and negative emotions. The ultimate nature of mind is pure, so there is a possibility of reducing the negative emotions and increasing the positive ones. Hence, there is the possibility to overcome suffering. Buddha explained this as the second Noble Truth. He explained karma and negative emotions, the true origin of suffering that is referred to as contaminated mind and contaminated karma. In order to truly understand the meaning of the second Noble Truth, one must delve into the meaning of true cessation, the third Noble Truth.

Buddha's first sermon explains the Four Noble Truths; the second sermon elaborates on the third Noble Truth. In the third sermon, there is a more profound explanation about the nature of mind, related with the fourth Noble Truth. Here there is both a possibility of reducing negative emotions as well as achieving permanent happiness. That is nirvana.

Once you understand the goal, only then can you eliminate the negative emotions. It is done through practice and the training of mind. In order to develop genuine tireless effort, we need determination. For that, it is extremely important to know the meaning of suffering. If there is a possibility as well as a goal to overcome suffering, it is worthwhile to think about and understand suffering. The more one realizes, the more determination one gains to overcome that suffering.

This is why the importance of the realization of renunciation is explained. There are two levels of that spirit of renunciation: the spirit of renunciation of the pleasures of this life and the spirit of renunciation of the pleasures of the next life. For example, when we think about the

sufferings in the six samsaric realms—the suffering of human beings, of animals and so forth—
and similarly about sufferings like old age,
sickness and death and so forth, we will be able to
generate a spirit of renunciation, or a wish to free
ourselves from cyclic existence, or samsara.

In order to generate a strong sense of renunciation toward the pleasures or attachments of the
next life, first it is important to have an understanding of the sufferings of the lower rebirths.
There is also another practical reason—the ultimate goal is Buddhahood, which we can achieve
through meditation and certain other practices.
It may take eons or it may take a thousand or a
hundred years. So for us to practice continually
we must be guaranteed a good rebirth in the next
life. Although our aim is Buddhahood, for practical reasons, while preparing for it, we shouldn't
neglect our future lives. Thus, while we are
planning long-term for Buddhahood, we must
fully prepare for the immediate prerequisites as
well.

Once you generate a spirit of renunciation
toward the attachments and pleasures of this
life, you naturally think about future pleasures
or generate some sort of attachment toward
the next life. That attachment has also to be

stopped gradually through the practice of the ten virtuous actions and by banishing the ten nonvirtuous actions. These fall under the first section of the *Lam-rim* teachings, which are mainly taught to people of lower-than-average intelligence.

To develop self-confidence, it is useful to meditate on the preciousness of human rebirth. With the help of the human body and human intelligence we can do everything if we make an effort. In the Bodhisattvayana, we have teachings regarding Buddha nature, *Buddhaseed,* the *sugatagarbha* or tathagatagarbha. This enlightened state, the ultimate nature that every sentient being possesses, proves that there is always the potential to eliminate negative emotions.

Thinking along these lines helps to develop self-confidence. A lot of people, especially in the West, have low self-esteem. I think that is very dangerous and really foolish. We have a body, our brain and wisdom. If we make an attempt through meditation and altruism, it is possible to develop our mind. With time and effort it can change. By constantly reminding ourselves of positivity and negativity, we can change things. Self-confidence, whether in religious practices or worldly life, is a very important element.

Compassion is a very crucial factor here. A more compassionate mind automatically opens some kind of inner door. It becomes very easy to communicate with fellow human beings, animals and insects. When our own attitude is open and there is nothing to hide, it immediately creates a basis for friendship. However, a negative emotion like fear closes that door. Unless you create that kind of groundwork yourself, it is very difficult to acquire genuine friends. Whether others respond or not, if you smile without suspicion and doubt, there is a greater chance of getting a smile in return.

Negative emotions negate this possibility. One then deliberately isolates oneself from the rest of humanity, and as a result, resentment, loneliness, fear, doubt, hopelessness and depression arise. Compassion, on the other hand, gives us inner strength. It opens our "inner door" and brings about better experiences.

The concept of Buddha nature, the concept of the preciousness of this life and this body are very important for developing self-confidence. We also have the teaching of impermanence, which is also very pertinent.

I want to mention here that very often people mistakenly believe that egoistic feelings are nega-

tive, that one should have no ego at all. I think
there are two types of ego, just as there are two
types of desire. Of the two types of feeling of "I,"
the feeling of "strong I" that forgets about others'
rights, and in which one considers oneself more
important than others, is wrong. The other type
of ego that makes one feel "I can do this, I can
help, I can serve" is positive. The bodhisattvas, I
think, have extraordinarily strong egos in that
sense.

This kind of ego develops tremendous determination in the people who possess it. For them
days, months, years are nothing. They count eons.
Not one or two eons, but millions, countless
eons. Such an inconceivably long time does not
discourage them, nor are they discouraged by the
countless sentient beings whose numbers are
limitless. Their determination is to do something
for an infinite number of sentient beings for an
infinite period of time. Such unshakable determination is impossible without a strong solid ego.
That ego is positive. It is necessary, useful and
constructive. We must develop it.

The other is the foolish ego which disregards
others' rights, forgets others and wants to gain
something by exploiting others. Now with that
kind of ego, ultimately one will lose and suffer.

Similarly, there are two kinds of desire. One is desire with a purpose that is good. This desire leads to determination. According to Buddhists, we ultimately reach Buddhahood because of this desire. The other desire is without a reason—a mere "I want this, I want that." This kind of desire without a proper basis very often leads to disaster. Some people get the impression that since the teachings identify desire as the source of all suffering, all desire is wrong. This is a misconception.

The next practice is impermanence. Here again, there are two levels. One impermanence is at the grosser level, like death or other misfortunes or when certain experiences change or end. The more subtle impermanence is that of momentary change. Modern physics has also explained this. For example, this flower in front of me is changing at a very subtle level, ever-changing in a wavelike fashion, like energy. This is subtle impermanence.

The realization of impermanence is very useful and important because you realize that it occurs simply through its own causes. Therefore, the disintegration or impermanent nature of phenomena does not depend on the need to encounter new causes and conditions. Due to their very nature of being produced by their causes and conditions, they are subject to disintegration and change.

Take the case of our body or our life. From the Buddhist point of view, there is no possibility of permanent happiness as long as everything is controlled, influenced or governed by ignorance. Once ignorance is eliminated, nirvana is achieved. As long as the same mind is influenced by ignorance, and as long as that situation lasts, that is samsara. As soon as ignorance is eliminated, suffering ceases. That is moksha, or liberation. Moksha, or salvation, is not a state of bliss or something external. It is an internal quality. Thus, the awareness of the deeper level of impermanence is very helpful in order to develop the desire or determination to achieve liberation. In this way when we think about the different levels of the nature of impermanence, we enter the second scope or second stage of practice of meditation on the path to Enlightenment. By reflecting on the meaning of the grosser level of impermanence, we generate a strong aspiration to achieve something better in the next life. And when we think about the nature of the subtle level of impermanence, we generate a strong aspiration to achieve nirvana.

Just as we are concerned for ourselves and think about ways to remove suffering and how to actualize nirvana and liberation and the state of ultimate happiness, if we turn our thoughts upon others and concern ourselves with the welfare of other sentient beings and reflect upon the removal of their suffering, we generate altruism or the wish to actualize Enlightenment for their benefit. That motivation is *bodhicitta*—the determination that is needed if we want to achieve Buddhahood.

It is quite marvelous that the human mind can generate this kind of determination or firm will. Once one develops such a precious mind of *bodhicitta,* irrespective of the religious context, one becomes extremely courageous, warmhearted and useful to society. According to the practice of Buddhist religion, *bodhicitta* is such a wonderful or marvelous quality that when we generate it, all negativities are purified and all positive qualities come alive. Once you generate such a precious mind, that mind ensures a good rebirth or good path in the future as well. In other words, it prepares you for the journey on the path to Enlightenment.

After that kind of determination comes the practice of the ten paramitas, or perfections, such as generosity, morality, patience, effort, concentration and wisdom. Of the ten paramitas, these are the six main perfections.

That is the way of Mahayana bodhisattva practice. In addition to that, we have the Tantrayana practice. If you further supplement this Mahayana practice with the practice of Tantrayana, then in Tantra there are Kriya Tantrayana, Carya Tantrayana, Yoga Tantrayana and Maha-Anuttara Yoga Tantrayana.

In tantric teaching, it is very important to visualize oneself as a deity—not mere visualization—one has to meditate on *shunyata,* or emptiness; then that wisdom is transformed at the level of one's imagination into the deity's form, Buddha's form. Furthermore, holding that form or Buddha's body as the subject, one reflects on the nature or the emptiness or suchness of it. So the profundity of the practice of tantra is undertaken through such practice. You reflect on the nature of the deity and at the same time on its ultimate nature. Thus, very powerful wisdom is combined with determination on the basis of *bodhicitta.* As a result, some wrathful acts also become very useful at times. Therefore, wrathful deities exist, and it is useful to make a distinction between anger and hatred, and love or compas-

sion and attachment. This is important. That is
the practice of tantra in general.

In Maha-Anuttara Yoga Tantrayana, one unique
practice is making a distinction among the gross,
subtle and innermost subtle levels of mind. There
are techniques to neutralize the grosser level of
mind after which the innermost subtle mind becomes active. That subtle mind, then, is transformed into wisdom, which is more powerful
than those wisdoms that are essentially in the category of grosser levels of mind. So that is the
Maha-Anuttara Yoga Tantrayana system. In Tibetan Buddhism you combine the basic teachings
of the Four Noble Truths with *bodhicitta* and the
six paramitas with deity yoga and certain kinds of
yoga practices. First you lay the foundation and
then build on it in order to reach the summit of
the practice. It is important to know that without the practice of Tantrayana or *bodhicitta* and
with only the practice of the Four Noble Truths
you can achieve liberation. On the other hand,
without a practice on the basis of the Four
Noble Truths, teaching just the ten paramitas or
Tantrayana is impossible.

Without Tantrayana, through Sutrayana alone,
we can practice and achieve a satisfactory result.
But the opposite—practicing only Tantrayana

without Sutrayana—makes it impossible to achieve a satisfactory result. The teachings are the ground floor, first floor, second floor, and so on, of a building. Without the ground floor it is impossible to build the first floor.

It is important to understand this because people are sometimes impatient and want Buddhahood immediately without considering the Four Noble Truths or the six paramitas. Deity practice, mandala and reciting alone will not work. We must go step by step.

Constitution Club Lawns, 1992

Compassion and

Nonviolence

I have no idea how to solve global crises, so it's better to talk on a practical level. Today, in addition to natural disasters, there are various man-made problems such as the events in Bosnia. In our daily news reports and on TV, we can see how much these innocent people suffer. In other parts of the world too, there is a great deal of killing, murder, even cases of children killing children. Sometimes people ask me, "What is your advice or suggestion?" I usually tell them I have no idea. These problems, I believe, are the result of long-standing negligence. These events did not come about suddenly. They have their causes and conditions. One cause and condition creates another cause, another condition and so on until things finally get out of hand. Most of these events are a result of human emotions out of control. When such calamities take place, it is very difficult to deal with them. Human emotion has to be combined with proper intelligence, which means intelligence with human affection. One can't be sure whether mere intelligence is destructive, or positive and constructive. Intelligence with affection, on the other hand, can produce marvelous results. Intelligence usually ceases to work when emotions are out of control. Nowadays many situations have reached that stage. If we ask certain individuals, even leaders, "What is your purpose in killing one another?" they may not have a clear answer. By killing, they simply let out their negative and blind emotions, inflicting heavy suffering on other people. So what is it we learn from these events?

In the future, if we want a happier humanity, a happy world, we must tackle the root of the problem. Of course the economy and political power are also causes. But the ultimate cause lies within the human mind. Every human action— verbal or physical—even a minor action, has some motivation. Ultimately everything depends upon our motivation. Proper motivation or proper development of motivation is an important factor.

Thus, if intelligence is accompanied with human affection and compassion—what I call human feeling, then it is very useful. The modern educational system pays too much attention to knowledge and to the brain and does not give enough attention to spiritual development. People leave it to religious organizations and others to take care of. I don't think that's sufficient. Although all world religions have the potential to make a tremendous contribution to the development of a good heart, even that's not sufficient. Moreover, many people feel that religion is something that is old-fashioned or out of date and religious people themselves are also at times a little too orthodox. They remain a little isolated from the real world and daily problems. Sometimes, many religious traditions, including the Tibetan tradition, place too much emphasis on ritual or ceremony without having a proper understanding of its meaning. Therefore the religious contribution and influence are also limited. It is not enough to let just religious communities handle moral issues. The problems are usually too big, and the group of people who are to handle the problems too small or too weak.

Take the case of the United States or some other countries. We can see clearly that they are facing some kind of moral crisis. They are either increasing their police force or seeking some other technical solution to their problems. Unless some positive developmental change occurs in each individual's heart, or unless there is some transformation there, it's very difficult to control external forces. Therefore each of us, as a part of the human community, has the responsibility to do something for humanity because if the future of humanity is good, bright and peaceful, we will all receive the benefit. If humanity degenerates morally, corruption, exploitation, bullying and cheating will all take place; as a result of this, society will suffer.

Although there are laws and regulations in each country, mischievous people always find ways around them. If society's moral values and standards of behavior become negative, each of us will suffer. Therefore the intentions of an individual are very much related to the interests of society. There is a definite correlation.

We should not think that the problem is a huge one and that the individual is too small. "My efforts will never have an effect on that immense problem" is not the right way to think. The problem may be big, but if every individual takes the initiative, then there is a real chance. If each individual remains isolated, neutral and indifferent, and expects dramatic change from others or from the sky or from meditation, that's ridiculous. Of course, prayer has its blessing and a limited effect. But the main effort must come from ourselves. Buddha and God have certainly had some kind of influence, but basically each individual has to make an effort with complete confidence. Whether we achieve satisfactory results or not, it is logical and worthwhile to make an attempt.

In spite of your constant effort, if you don't achieve the desired result, is doesn't matter. At least you will not have regrets. When unfortunate events occur due to our negligence, it is far worse and regrettable. Therefore each of us must realize our potential and make the effort.

I have spent most of my life outside my own country as a refugee. Many Tibetans trust me; they have great expectations and my task or responsibility is very great. There have been a lot of difficulties. Throughout this period, in spite of the many difficulties and problems, it seems to me that when I compare my experiences with those of other people, I am quite a happy person.

Of course, when there is bad news or something tragic happens, I experience anxiety, sadness and frustration, but that does not remain for long. In spite of the circumstances, my mind remains relatively stable and peaceful. This has helped me a great deal and enabled my wisdom and intelligence to function normally without much disturbance and so I sleep without any difficulties. And since my mind remains comparatively calm, my digestion and health are fine. As a result I get many benefits. A lot of Tibetans who experienced intense torture and other difficulties and lost their families have been able to maintain their mental stability and calm. Over the last four years, we have had occasional meetings with scientists, psychologists, neurobiologists and physicists. When we discussed mental problems and tried to understand and explain them, some of these scientists were really surprised. Some Tibetans had suffered terribly but their mental states have remained remarkably calm and stable.

What is this inner strength that enables one to maintain calm in the face of difficulties? It is not the result of external factors, medicines, injections, drugs or alcohol. Nor some kind of external blessing. Inner strength stems from true training of the mind.

Regardless of whether one is a believer, through mind training one can shape one's attitude. As a result, a person becomes calmer and more at peace, and able to handle difficult, urgent and even the most complicated matters better. Past experience and discussion with other experienced people also contribute to the smooth handling of problems. There's no doubt then, that problems at the family, community and even international levels can be reduced if they are man-made.

The educational system and family life are two very important areas. In the educational field, one has to take care not only of the brain, but also of one's spiritual development. I say "spiritual development" not in a religious sense but simply in the sense of having a good and compassionate heart. If one has a compassionate heart, it automatically brings inner strength and allows for less fear and less doubt. Subsequently, one becomes happier and more open-minded, thus making more friends in society. When we consider education from the teacher's point of view, it is quite clear that teachers must impress upon the minds of students the value and effect of human affection through their conduct and actions.

On the other hand, it is important to limit the size of a family through birth control measures. It is essential to have fewer children, only as many as we can properly take care of. Apart from education, one must instill in them the value of human life and affection.

The media is another important area. In modern times, the media often spells trouble, but generally it is very useful. In democratic countries particularly, freedom of the press is extremely useful. Freedom of the press enables them to sort out scandals and curb corruption. It is important to put forward a balanced view in the media—to portray both the negative and positive aspects. Very often newspaper reports focus on the negative things—murder, rape, robbery and so on—and do not carry sufficient coverage of positive issues. There is hardly any news of how many children or how many sick people receive the benefit of human kindness and affection. An overdose of negativity leads the general public to believe that human nature is basically negative, and that idea ultimately leads to a great deal of frustration. One also loses self-confidence. This is both tragic and dangerous. So the media plays an important role, and religious people have their special responsibility in this context. From every angle, and through various professions, one must promote the value of the compassionate mind. Although it is not easy, it is the only way toward a better humanity and a happier future.

I shall now explain something about the method of Buddhist practice. First I would like to stress the importance of harmony among different religions. In spite of differing philosophies, all the major world religions have a similar message, and similar advice, for humanity. There are some extraordinary persons who follow different religions who have totally transformed their inner state. As a result, they are truly compassionate and wise. This implies that all these different traditions have the potential to produce such inner transformation in the human mind. So, whether we like it or not, these major religions will always remain. In the past, many people have benefited from these traditions, and the same holds true for the present and the future as well. Therefore, it is extremely important to have genuine harmony among the religious traditions. It is possible since there is a common ground. And once we know more about other traditions, we automatically develop more respect and appreciation for them. Genuine mutual understanding leads to mutual respect. As far as Buddhism is concerned, it involves the training of the mind.

Buddhism emphasizes the training and transformation of mind because all events are the result of one's actions. We call that karma. Our future depends on today's actions. That is the law of karma, or the law of causality. Of verbal, mental and physical actions, mental action is supreme. Mental motivation is the key factor.

The same verbal or physical actions can at times be positive and at other times negative because of different mental motivations. In some cases, with certain motivation, actions that are normally considered negative can actually become positive. Mental action is thus superior, and the critical factor, and all events ultimately depend upon our own mind. The ultimate goal is moksha, or liberation. Moksha is a mental state where all grosser mental afflictive emotions are completely eradicated. Moksha or nirvana is a mental quality.

And finally we have Buddhahood. Once the mind and awareness are fully developed and awakened without any obstacles, the state of Buddha's mind is reached: that which we call Enlightenment. That is also a mental quality. The subject to be transformed is the mind, the transformer is also the mind, and the resultant transformed state is the mind as well. Some people describe Buddhism as a science of the mind. It seems appropriate to explain it thus.

There are a lot of explanations in Buddhism about the nature of mind at the conventional and ultimate level, and a distinction is made between different kinds of mental thought. Tantrayana makes a very precise distinction between different levels of mind: gross, more subtle and innermost subtle. Since the method to transform the mind is in itself of the nature of mind, meditation becomes a very important part of Buddhist practice.

You cannot change your mind without meditation. There are two kinds of meditation—analytical and single-pointed. The actual weapon against negativity is analytical meditation. Through analysis one can develop a new conviction or awareness. As this awareness increases, opposing forces are reduced. Analytical meditation destroys negativity. *Vipassana,* or special insight, is a particular kind of analytical meditation. In order to stabilize that analytical meditation, a forceful, single-pointed meditation is crucial. Our mind is usually so scattered that when we want to analyze something, we use the energy of only a part of our mind. A lot of energy is wasted. Through *shamatha,* single-pointed meditation, we channel all the energy of the mind. We unify it like hydroelectric energy. When water is sprinkled it can't move forcefully; when the same amount of water is channeled, its energy or force increases. Our mind is scattered, and yet by nature it has the capacity for knowledge. But because it is so scattered, its effect is very limited. Therefore it is necessary to channel the energy of the mind through *shamatha* meditation.

Analytical meditation itself is of two kinds. One is like compassion or faith. Mind itself is transformed into the nature of karuna, or compassion. The other analytical meditation is like understanding impermanence and emptiness as objects to be realized. There are many kinds of meditation, but these two are important and relevant aspects of Buddhist practice.

One also needs to keep in mind the aspect of motivation. In bodhisattvayana, the key factor that motivates all action, even worldly action, is the motivation to attain the path that leads to Buddhahood. For that, the key factor is *bodhicitta,* the mind of infinite altruism. (Altruism here refers to the wish to attain Buddhahood for the sake of all sentient beings.) So with this motivation, the different types of meditation actually lead to Buddhahood.

It is not possible to plunge into high meditation, which is very difficult to achieve or implement. As Aryadeva states in his four hundred verses, our goal, Buddhahood, means complete elimination of all negative stains of mind including the imprints or predispositions called "obscurations" to Buddhahood. The practice must proceed step by step. In order to eliminate these imprints of the delusions, first we have to eliminate all the mental defilements. As a first step, we need *shila,* disciplined moral conduct. Whether one is a monk or layman, there is no difference in this respect that the first principle is *shila.* The main thing is to abandon the ten nonvirtues: the physical ones—killing, stealing and sexual misconduct; the verbal ones—lying, divisive speech, harsh talk and idle gossip; and the mental ones—covetousness, harmful intention and wrong views.

Wrong views have two interpretations. One is nihilism, not accepting the existence of anything, and the other is the extreme of exaggeration, accepting things as having independent existence. In order to practice moral conduct and self-discipline, the key factor is constant mindfulness in our daily life. When we are about to talk to someone, we should constantly check whether we are about to lie or not. And in our daily life, we should constantly check our physical, verbal and mental actions.

Sometimes, in a particular situation, one might have to be slightly deceitful. In order to save the lives of many people, for example, it is permissible to tell a small lie. Except for such cases, one must be very truthful and honest. At times, we are far too polite, and this creates suspicion. Honest, open and beautiful speech always carries some weight. One should be kind and refrain from harming others. In this context, vegetarianism is extremely good. I myself tried to become vegetarian in the early sixties and remained a strict vegetarian for about two years. However, I developed some physical problems, which is why I am not a vegetarian anymore. These days, I am vegetarian on alternate days, so, effectively, for six months of the year I am vegetarian. Recently while driving from Dharamsala to Jammu airport, I noticed a lot of chickens in tiny boxes. It was a terrible sight. Those who live in coastal regions survive on fish—thousands of fish are killed every day. In order to satisfy one human stomach, so many lives are taken away. We must promote vegetarianism. It is extremely important. I really feel that our human population should be reduced. We should save the lives of other species. Smaller numbers signify friendlier and happier people and since the cause of much social illness is poverty, world economy is a crucial factor.

Sexual misconduct is one of the main factors responsible for destroying the peace of the family and humanity at large. Sexual self-discipline is greatly required. Especially now, when all over the world we have this terrible disease known as AIDS.

If moral self-discipline is practiced, the quality of life becomes better and one is a happier person whom others respect. These practices not only lead to ultimate happiness, but immediately create a very positive atmosphere in our family and community; and the individual, too, is happier. On the surface, the life of a nun or monk seems unattractive. The layman's life appears more attractive and colorful. Our lives may seem less colorful, but in the long run I think the mental state of nuns and monks is more balanced.

Undisciplined people have a very colorful life—sometimes too happy, at others too frustrated (their life is like a yo-yo). This isn't good for the body. A calm and steady mental state is more desirable. By practicing restraint, we also make a tremendous contribution toward harmless birth control. This is moral conduct on a daily basis.

Our real enemies are negative human emotions such as hatred, jealousy and pride—the real destroyer of our future and our happiness. It is very difficult to fight this enemy without taking proper defensive measures.

Self-discipline, although difficult, and not always easy while combating negative emotions, should be a defensive measure. At least we will be able to prevent the advent of negative conduct dominated by negative emotion. That is *shila,* or moral ethics. Once we develop this by familiarizing ourselves with it, along with mindfulness and conscientiousness, eventually that pattern and way of life will become a part of our own life.

Shila is the basis on which you directly engage with negative emotions. When you have a strong body, your hand is strong and steady and you can effectively use the ax to cut a tree. *Shila* is like that energetic and strong body. With a strong and steady hand, you can hit your target repeatedly on the same spot. Samadhi is like that hand. And wisdom is the ax that actually cuts the tree.

What then is *vipassana*? There are many varieties of *vipassana*—meditation on death, impermanence and many other connected meditations. According to bodhisattvayana, the main *vipassana* meditation is the wisdom that arises from analytical meditation that realizes and meditates on the ultimate nature of oneself, others and all phenomena. That is *shunya.*

In order to realize *shunya,* we must first be attentive to the differences between appearance and reality. Very often there are contradictions, things that appear one way while reality may be quite different. When we talk about *shunya*—ultimate nature that we call nothingness—it is the absence of independent existence. But to our sense organs, and to the brain, everything appears as if it exists by itself—independently existent. If things truly exist as they appear, then they should get clearer through analytical meditation. But, if we investigate, we cannot find them. There is a difference between appearance and reality. In order to make that clear, Buddhist literature speaks of the two truths: conventional truth and ultimate truth.

The possibility of ultimate nature is made clear when we study the two truths. The realization of ultimate truth or ultimate nature of all phenomena directly influences negative emotions, because generally all negative emotions are based on the construct that things exist independently. Such a conception acts as the basis for all negative emotions. That is the second level—the direct engagement, combating and controlling the inner enemies that are the negative emotions.

When you gain victory over these emotions,

that is the stage of liberation, moksha or nirvana. Once you win in this offensive act, it still does not mean that everything is fully under control. A few snipers may still exist. So, in order to eliminate all these sniperlike imprints of negative emotions, we require a lot of effort. At this stage, motivated by *bodhicitta,* we engage in the six or ten paramitas, or perfections, and further promote the realization of *shunyata.* This is the bodhisattva's way of practice.

Now it is obvious that the practice must be carried out step by step. Here we need more patience. When we explain Buddhahood or moksha, sometimes people get very excited. And when we elaborate that in order to reach that goal we have to go step by step, people sometimes lose patience. That is not positive. I think that in some cases, we Tibetans lack seriousness. We know Buddhism very well, but in terms of practice we are sometimes lazy. Some of our new Buddhists, especially from the West, are very, very serious—sometimes a bit too serious. After a few years, they lose interest in it completely! Seriousness is good, but only if accompanied by patience. Without patience, it tends to bring disaster.

Cleansing all the imprints of negative emotions is rather difficult. This is where tantra, especially Maha-Anuttarayoga tantra teachings, is involved. But that is not easy at all, as a special quality is required at that level.

Whether believers or not, we are human beings first. And as human beings we have the wonderful capacity to know the positive and negative consequences in the long term as well as the short term. Morally, we have the great responsibility of looking after not only fellow human beings but other species of animals, other sentient beings, and our environment as well. Therefore, we should try to lead good, qualified, worthy human lives, be good human beings, and more warmhearted persons. This will automatically bring more happiness to our individual life and to our family and community. It automatically benefits oneself as well as others.

Those of us who consider ourselves Buddhists should practice the dharma sincerely and not be contented merely with the intellectual level. Implement it in daily life with constant effort; time is a very important and major factor. If we expect great things right in the beginning, great spiritual change in the mind within a short period, it is not a healthy sign. We must count eons. It really gives us inner strength. Our scriptures tell us that in three years we can achieve Buddhahood. I think this is impractical. Sometimes there is a bit of exaggeration here and there, but even if we truly believe, I don't think we can achieve Buddhahood in three years even if we are like Milarepa who was such a strong and determined person with an indestructible heart. Of all our great yogis, saints and practitioners, I haven't heard of anyone who has achieved Buddhahood within three years.

So, asking for three years is not enough. We must plan well, not only for this year, not only for this life, but for life after life, centuries and eons. When I think about eons, great, countless eons, it really makes me genuinely calm, and I get real inner strength.

❦

What is happiness and what is life? What is Enlightenment?
According to one's own experience, one feels satisfied, calm and happy. Happiness is happiness! Everybody is trying to achieve it.

Plants have life, but I am not sure if they have feeling or not. We, on the other hand, experience pain and pleasure. When we talk about sentient beings, we refer to beings that have life as well as these painful and pleasurable experiences.

Enlightenment, as I mentioned briefly before, is total knowledge—no ignorance and no obstacles. Our subtle mind—what we call the clear light—has every potential to become enlightened and fully awakened. But now, because of ignorance, there are many obstacles in the face of full awakening. When all the negative factors disappear, the power or force of awareness is fully developed and that is what we call Enlightenment.

Is it possible to bear somebody else's karma for that person?

Generally speaking, according to Buddhist teaching, you will not encounter the results of an action that you have not committed, and once you have committed an action, the result will never get lost, and you have to experience it. Here I think it's quite important to make a distinction. When you suffer, you feel not only pain or discomfort at that moment, but also a kind of helplessness and discouragement. You are completely enshrouded in that suffering and there is a kind of darkness. Compassion is when you have concern for others' suffering, and share their suffering on the basis that others have an equal right to be happy. The suffering at that moment may make you unhappy or cause a little discomfort, but that discomfort is voluntarily accepted with reason because of these realizations and the decision to share others' suffering. Therefore the discomfort and unease leave no trace of darkness on your mind. You have to be very clear, and very alert if you voluntarily take on others' suffering.

In vipassana *meditation, what sort of transformation takes place when one's attention moves from one part to another part of the body?*

There are many varieties of *vipassana* meditation. As far as I know, there is one type of *vipassana* meditation regarding the body. When we have attachment, we have a clear concept of "my body" and at that time we identify with it. We feel that an independent body exists. If we meditate on different parts of the body, eventually the feeling of a solid body or something very precious disappears. "My body" begins to signify many different particles and combinations. Once you realize that, your feeling of solidity, oneness and preciousness no longer exists.

Mindfulness of the body involves meditation on different parts of the body. The most important and powerful *vipassana* is the meditation on *shunyata,* or emptiness.

A personal question: I failed a lot in life, but at every step my father helped me. He told me that I should become a better person from my failures. For a couple of months I became very calm, I did not lose my temper much, but now that I have a job and success in life, I have started losing my temper. I want to achieve something in life. Is it wrong?

That's difficult to answer. I don't know what your basic belief is, or your attitude toward life and toward past and future lives. I am not sure about your lifestyle. There would be different remedies depending on your attitude to your own life. Generally, whenever something negative arises, I always try to remember that other people also have more or less similar experiences. Thinking that way releases some of my mental burden. Also, I always try to find some positive aspect of that negative circumstance. Sometimes, this perspective allows one a more positive and creative experience. Thus, the nature of an event is relative. An event can have different aspects and if we look closely, we may find something positive. It may not be positive in itself, but it may decrease our frustration.

Self-confidence is important. Human beings have a wonderful brain and determination. Buddhists speak of Buddha nature, *Buddhaseed*. Even without discussing these things, we have the potential to achieve them; if we utilize our intelligence with greater patience and constant effort, even if we fail the first three times, there is still a possibility of ultimately achieving the goal.

Maybe not in three years, but many teachers say the realization of the absolute can happen in an instant, as opposed to through a long path. Please comment.

It does happen sometimes, but only with many causes and conditions. In some cases it happens at an invisible level. When causes and conditions are fully ripe, then it occurs instantly. Certain extraordinary spiritual experiences do take place.

When all religions teach compassion, love and brotherhood, how is it that human beings are fighting in the name of religion, especially on our continent?

In most cases individuals are simply happy to label themselves. For instance, I can say, "I'm a Buddhist," and be content with it. People don't bother about their daily practice, conduct or thinking; they don't bother to go deeper into the meaning. Buddhism in my case is supposed to guide me and my conduct. It is both a way of thinking and behavior as well as the means to reshape these. But sometimes one doesn't regard it that seriously. So if I have no intention of changing according to Buddhist ideals, but continue to use Buddhism claiming it as "my religion," then I am utilizing Buddhism because I need religious strength.

Similarly, when you say, "I am a Christian," you invoke all Christianity as your support. And you are never touched by that tradition and are never changed. When a totally ignorant, frustrated or hateful person uses religion, it is a disaster. What you should do is check yourself, consider yourself a practitioner and a sincere follower of that tradition. It is only then that you will become a different individual.

There are certain sincere practitioners who, out of ignorance and lack of contact, believe only in their own religion and consider other religions wrong. In some cases it is the result of teaching, but usually it is due to lack of contact, lack of awareness and real understanding of the deeper value of the other tradition. Once you realize that there are wonderful people among Christians and Muslims, you automatically develop an appreciation for their tradition.

The follower of each religion should check for oneself, whether he or she is following it sincerely or not, and whether it is being practiced genuinely. Constant communication or exchange with other religions is required. This morning at the seventh World Religion Conference in Delhi, I mentioned that in order to develop genuine harmony, there should be constant meetings first among the leaders, second among the scholars, and third among those people who have deeper experiences. Meetings between these people are essential. Once you know each other's deeper values and the potential for the negative in the human mind, once you know each other, it is very helpful.

How can compassion be generated or developed in one's life and how can it be practiced?
Through analytical as well as single-pointed meditation. Analytical meditation involves the constant examination of the value of compassion. Once you become a more compassionate person, you have real conviction. You become a calmer and happier person, have less fear and more self-confidence; you become more open-minded and have better communication with other people; you gain more friends and more smiles. On the other hand, examine hatred—what is its value?

Hatred destroys one's own happiness, one's family's happiness as well as happiness at the na-

tional and international levels. If you are to remain in a three-year retreat and you meditate on
hatred, you will never experience calmness, you
will always feel uncomfortable and eventually
you will lose your appetite, your sleep and your
life. That is what hatred does. So, you see, like a
scientist we must try to examine the positive and
negative aspects of these things constantly. Try to
get rid of the negative aspects and promote or
produce positive qualities through analysis.

Similarly, when we talk about the mind, it is
not just one single entity. There are many, many
thoughts and many, many minds. Some are positive, like medicine. Some are negative and are
much, much worse than even poison.

As in material things you retain certain positive aspects and discard others, so it is with the
mind. Those minds that bring us more happiness,
calm or inner strength and friends are positive.
Minds that eventually destroy these things are obviously negative. So, analyze these things. Once
you get some kind of conviction and full ascer-
tainment, through analytical meditation, ponder
on it for a short while. If you are a believer, recite
some mantras. That is the way—some analytical
meditation, then at the end, single-pointed meditation. When the force of that conviction

reduces, engage yourself in analytical meditation again.

If one is in great anguish and realizes it as the effect of past karma, but cannot bear the suffering, what should one do? Can prayer help?
According to some traditions like Buddhism, confession of negative actions is one method. The Tibetan Buddhist Tantrayana tradition recommends recitation of different mantras, making certain images or relics, and many religions have the practice of generosity. In addition, one should pray.

Is it possible or advisable to show compassion to someone who continues to harm or hurt you?
Oh yes, of course! That is most important! The enemy or the other person who is trying to harm or is harming you—although that person's attitude toward you is negative—is after all a human being and also has the right to overcome suffering and achieve happiness. On that basis you have to cultivate compassion toward that person. That does not mean that you just bow down in front of your enemy. There are different reasons—reasons enough to feel compassion, and also, in some cases, sufficient reason to confront the enemy. These are two different things.

*Why should we try to eliminate suffering? Is it not an
essential part of life as much as happiness?*
If you are satisfied with daily life with all its suffering, then that is best. You do not need to worry
or make an effort.

*Could His Holiness please describe his visit to Baba
Amte's project? What can we learn from Baba's practical form of compassion?*
Practical compassion—I believe that is the proper
way to develop India. Having just a few industries
near cities is not enough. Of course, it is both
good and necessary and a part of development,
but real transformation and change of India
should come through the works of people like
Baba Amte—work that is done at the grassroots
level. I am particularly impressed by the new
colony. I was told that it was just empty, uninhab-
ited land earlier. Now it has been transformed
into a small village full of human spirit and self-
confidence. When I was there, a patient who had
only two fingers was using a hammer very forcefully. I think because I was there, his force was
even stronger. I was a little worried that his hammer may hit his own hand. That place was full of
life and the people had no feeling of inferiority,
only a sense of equality. We shook hands without

any hesitation. It was all very wonderful, very beautiful. I was greatly impressed.

Why do we come to this world?
Nature is nature. There is no answer.

You said that proper development of motivation is the key factor. How do we develop that motivation?
I think as I have already explained—through training of the mind, through analysis based upon one's own past experience, to examine one's past as well as the past experiences of others, like Mahatma Gandhi, or Baba Amte. When I met Baba Amte, in spite of his physical difficulties, he had a smile on his face, he was full of life, full of spirit and radiant. That is the result of compassion and self-confidence. People like Hitler and Mao Tse-tung had such tremendous power, but they were full of suspicion and hatred. I think Mao was quite a sophisticated person—full of confidence—but he was suspicious of even his best comrades. Once there is such suspicion and hatred, a person cannot be happy. Therefore, compassion is important because all of us want to be happy in life.

What is the best method to stop the population growth? Does Buddhist philosophy have a role to play?

More monks and more nuns, of course! I call it nonviolent birth control. It is necessary.

On the eve of your first visit to Jerusalem, what is your message on interreligious relations?
A few years ago I started a practice that I consider a step toward establishing harmony among religions: a pilgrimage to different holy places with a group of people from different religions. We go together and pray together in silence, and it is quite an experience. I started with Sarnath. Last year at Trivandrum, in Kerala, I got the opportunity to visit a mosque, a church and a Ganesh temple. I saw a beautiful silver Ganesh. I thought Ganesh had a very nice stomach; after that visit, I thought I would make some money, but I didn't. Anyway, I loved that Ganesh. At the mosque I had my first opportunity to pray together with our Muslim brothers. This I really feel is a powerful method to communicate with people from different religious traditions. I saw Jerusalem many years ago, after which I have been very eager to go to holy places like Jerusalem.

Recently I visited Lourdes in France—where the vision of Mary appeared. It was truly wonderful. I am not a Christian, I am a Buddhist. And in that way I am a nonbeliever. I do not believe in

God. We Buddhists do not accept a creator. Nevertheless, I deeply respect and appreciate the Christian tradition and all other religions. Therefore, when I was there, I felt a deep satisfaction. It was quite wonderful. If possible, I will go to Mecca as well, but I don't know when. I am really looking forward to going to Jerusalem with a group of people from different religious traditions.

If we are all human beings, what is the difference between you and me?
I think there is a great difference. You are you and I am me!

Modern School, Barakhamba, 1994

How to Live and Die

in a Better Way

I will interpret on three levels how to live and die happily. First, for the nonbeliever, then for the general believer, and finally for the Buddhist practitioner.

I believe that all of us survive on the expectation and hope of happiness. None of us wants to suffer. The purpose of our life is the attainment of happiness. One can achieve happiness at the physical and mental level, as well as at the level at which one can alleviate or abate suffering. There can be two types of happiness: the happiness one gets from achieving happiness mentally and physically and the happiness that can be attained through the decrease of suffering.

Death signifies suffering and is definitely something that we do not desire. However, if we are able to learn how to face death, that preparation ensures that we do not have to experience great suffering. Being able to encounter death in a relaxed way and without unhappiness is dependent on how you live your daily life. When you are alive, if you are able to control your mind, calmness becomes a habit; so, when you actually encounter death, you can face it in a relaxed way. If our daily life is meaningful and positive, at the time of death we can feel "during my whole lifetime, at least I did something meaningful. Although I wish to remain in this world a little longer, I have no regrets."

You may ask what it means to lead a meaningful day-to-day life. Whether we are believers or not, it is a reality that we are all living. If we examine the purpose of our life, we will be able to realize that our life is not meant to create disturbance but to bring more harmony and happiness. We are social creatures. Our life is not dependent on one cause and condition but on several causes and conditions. If we are able to understand that our life is multifaceted and dependent on many causes and conditions, this realization will enable us to lead our life in a more meaningful manner. No matter how strong an individual is, we have to live as a human community. If someone lives in isolation, he will eventually experience a lot of mental frustration because it is human nature to be social. Many of our needs, such as sufficient food and shelter, are provided by the efforts of others. So the happiness and comfort in our daily life depends greatly on others. That's the reality, and our daily life or way of thinking should be according to these conditions and factors. Human intelligence is so sophisticated that it sometimes creates an image that hides the reality. Sometimes one is under the false illusion that one is independent and capable of achieving anything, and one does not realize how much one's life is dependent on the existence, help and support of others. This applies not only to people but also to the environment and other species—in fact, to everything. A lot of problems and suffering are caused because one is unable to realize the help and support one receives from the surrounding environment, and because one does not pay proper attention and understand their importance.

Even though your focus may be on your personal happiness and well-being, once you are able to understand how much your personal life is dependent on the surrounding environment, you will be able to widen your perspective and your realization of reality. This widened perspective will enable you to create a more harmonious life, not only for yourself but for others as well.

That kind of wider perspective or view then

automatically results in a sense of commitment and concern for others. This is not for reasons holy or sacred, but because one's own future depends on these factors. This view is not only realistic but is also the basis of secular moral ethics. We lie, cheat and perform many other negative deeds toward other members of our community on which our future depends. Due to our short-sightedness or ignorance, we manipulate the very factors on which our future depends. The realization of this results in a more compassionate and helpful attitude. It helps in developing a compassionate mental attitude, and nonviolence is the best way to solve the problems facing humanity. Using force means denying the rights of others. Nonviolence, on the other hand, is a human approach and a meaningful way of human dialogue. A meaningful human dialogue can be achieved only through mutual respect or mutual understanding in a spirit of reconciliation.

Once you are able to cultivate this kind of perspective and attitude and are able to treat each individual thusly, you will be able to make your daily life meaningful.

When I summarize this, I tell people that we should always try to help others as much as possible, and even if we are unable to help them, we must at least refrain from harming them. This is a summary of the Buddhist philosophy, which is relevant even to nonbelievers. In the long run, if individuals remain more compassionate, they will be happier. Through negative activities, one can gain temporarily, but deep down there is always some kind of dissatisfaction.

When I talk about the necessity and importance of cultivating compassion, I do not for once advocate taking a passive stand. In modern competitive society there are many occasions where we need to take a tough stand. By cultivating our motivation and compassionate attitude to benefit other people, we create positive thinking and attitudes that help us take the tough stand that is required.

At the actual time of dying, a calm mind is essential. The friends or those looking after the dying person should also have a calm mind. Even though they have sincere motivation and want to help, their actions sometimes create more agitation and disturbance in the mind of a dying person.

Now for the second level—the believers. Although I am not competent to explain the various philosophies, I feel it is good that people believe in the creator and are God-fearing. One wants certain things, but one knows they are against God's wish or will; this type of control is very useful in developing a positive attitude. Then there is the question of compassion and love. Sometimes the opportunity to do negative things exists, but because of respect and desire to be a faithful follower, one refrains from doing them. This is a very good way of self-improvement. The genuine expression of loving God is to love thy neighbor. I think that a person who shows genuine loving kindness, love and compassion to his brothers and sisters sincerely loves God. Some people weep in front of images of Christ or other deities, but in daily life and dealings, that faith and genuine compassion is missing. Genuine compassion and faith in a God can lessen anxiety. But this does not mean that one puts all responsibility on God. God shows you the way, but you also have the great responsibility to implement and follow faithfully.

At the time of death you should remember Allah or God or some other figure. I think this is one way to reduce mental tension or worry. That is why I believe that all major world religions have equal and great potential to help humanity—reduce mental frustrations, for example— and all major world religions give us hope. When we are faced with physical retardation or other problems at the beginning of our life, there seems to be not much hope. In spite of that, however, there is something to be hopeful for in the future that lies ahead.

For my interpretation on the third level to the Buddhists—What is a meaningful and positive life? What are the demarcations? Innately, we long for happiness and do not want suffering. This is a law of nature. If you ask why we have this desire, the Buddhist explanation is that all the negative experiences are temporary and can be eliminated. Because there is a Buddha nature, a *Buddhaseed,* within us, all these negative emotions can be eliminated. Every sentient being has the potential of Buddha nature. From birth every sentient being has the desire for happiness and wants relief from suffering. On that basis, those actions and motivations that bring satisfaction or happiness are positive, and those that ultimately bring suffering are negative.

How do you live in a better way? The essential thing, as I mentioned earlier, is to help others. If more people are smiling, you get peace. If more people look sad, you also feel sad. I saw some people who were not very old, but they looked old—a mother, father and a small daughter. They were selling newspapers and had very sad faces.

Seeing them really made me very sad. If you create more smiles, you get more happiness. You achieve immediate satisfaction and in the long run you gain more reliable friends. However, friends made by money are not genuine friends. Only friends made through human affection are genuine.

If you can help, then help. If you cannot, at least refrain from harming others. Why should we restrain ourselves from harming others? The reason is our interdependence. Our future depends on others. Even an individual's mental happiness is dependent on many factors and conditions. Today's experience is the result of the causes and effects of yesterday as well as the experiences in our previous lives and so on. The whole universe, the entire galaxy, comes and goes in this manner. According to modern theory, the world came into existence with a big bang and it will ultimately dissolve. If that is the case, then we Buddhists have to think more seriously. But then, there are several big bangs, one after another. Therefore, according to cosmology, the Buddhist theory fits very well. All this is due to action and motivation based on the law of cause and effect: everything is momentarily changing and depends on causes and conditions.

The momentary changes that take place in all impermanent phenomena are dependent on individual causes and conditions. These causes of momentary changes do not come from nonconcordant causes and conditions, nor do they take place without causes and conditions. When we talk of momentary changes dependent on causes and conditions, there are two categories of causes: the cooperative and the substantial.

Whatever is not long-lasting, whatever is subjected to disintegration, which includes the bodhisattvas and enlightened Buddhas who are impermanent, will change and disintegrate. Even in the state of Buddhahood, among the Buddha's qualities, we find that some are impermanent while others are permanent. Thus all phenomena, be they permanent or impermanent, even in the stage of Buddhahood, are subject to change and disintegration. Even the karma theory is dependent on the theory of causality. Such changes are not just created by the mind. The meaning of practice is to first know the reality, and then according to the reality develop the method that is suitable to it. That is the process of changing the mind.

Therefore, when we talk about carrying out certain spiritual practices, we are talking about a way of life, following a practice that is in tune with the nature of how things exist. When we do certain practices in harmony with nature, it is extremely important to first understand how things exist, the law of nature—as it is also from this point of view that the teaching of the Buddha develops. Likewise, the Buddha also taught the use of methods of investigation based on the reality and nature of phenomena. In the teaching of the Buddha, great importance is given to the concept of valid perception. This is so important because it is through valid perception that we are able to understand nature.

When we understand the law of nature and the importance of knowing how things exist, then while we actually carry out the practices, we realize how significant it is to transform our mind stage by stage. Even the same kind of mind focusing on the same kind of object can be transformed gradually by removing the wrong state of mental level and finally leading it to the state of valid perception. For example, we may have a completely perverted idea about a particular object. A true study and investigation can transform that wrong understanding into a doubt, then gradually turn the doubt more toward a fact that could be gradually turned into a correct assumption, then into inferential cognition, and finally it can be transformed into a valid perception allowing the understanding of that particular object.

Therefore, understanding how things actually exist, and being able to distinguish between appearance and reality, is extremely important. To reduce the disparity between reality and appearance, it is best to know the truth. When we lay so much importance on the understanding of how things actually exist, we are doing so not merely for the sake of understanding alone, but because we want happiness and do not want suffering. We can cultivate and achieve happiness, remove and eliminate suffering, provided we are able to engage in a practice that is in tune with the law of nature and in tune with how things actually exist. It is because of this that the Buddha taught the Four Noble Truths.

Because our objective is the attainment of happiness or some kind of permanent happiness eventually, we have to take every care of the causes and conditions of that goal. This is the basic reason why we should follow nonviolence based on compassion. In other words, if we cannot help others, we should refrain from harming them. Why should we do this? We have to engage in the practice of nonviolence and compassion

because of the reality of our interdependence
with all other sentient beings.

From early morning, when our mental state is
fresh and alert, we should cultivate a positive
mental attitude, not just through wishing but
through analytical meditation. Analyze and investigate the benefit of a positive mental attitude,
and the suffering or disadvantage of a negative attitude. That is what we call analytical meditation.
Analytical meditation is more powerful than
single-minded meditation. Also, in the beginning, and in a simple way, try to keep in mind infinite altruism. Then, with that motivation, do
more detailed and analytical meditations on impermanence or the different experiences of reality, then impermanence again, and if you can, and
have the interest, investigate ultimate reality.

Compassion is the method, and wisdom the
philosophical view of understanding reality. The
combination of wisdom and motivation is the
proper way to transform your mental attitude.
There is bound to be some kind of emotion like
anger or attachment, due to past dispositions. If
you investigate and develop positive counter-
forces, those negative emotions will start disinte-
grating. Other kinds of emotions are a strong
sense of altruism and compassion. These are not

the result of past dispositions, but due to the analysis of the benefits and disadvantages of the emotions. In this way you develop these motivations. The positive emotions can be developed through analytical meditation. The two sides, the wisdom side and the method side, must be combined. If you try to develop this positive motivation from early morning, you create more positive feelings, and the whole day you retain some influence of the morning practice. Then at least one day, even though it is not a perfect one, is less negative. The next day also, try to remember "I must have a meaningful day." Continue in this manner day by day, week by week. At the beginning, it is really uncontrollable, but as time passes, and with constant effort and determination, eventually you will feel a new hope. You can do it.

Cultivating all these positive forces is possible, for it is our basic nature, and the negative things will automatically reduce and weaken. It is possible to totally eliminate these negative things. It is not easy and may involve several eons. However, it is better to think of eons than a few years. Some practitioners go into a three-year retreat with great expectations. You go into retreat as a normal person and expect to come out a great bodhisattva. That is, I think, highly unrealistic. So it is better to count eons rather than just a few years. My own experience is that too many expectations right at the beginning, later become a source of disappointment and failure. From the very beginning you need more determination, and it does not matter if it takes eons. When it comes to doing something that is right, time does not matter as long as every day of our life becomes useful. That is the purpose—time is not important. If it is a painful experience, time matters; but if it is a joyful experience, it does not. Then, even a longer time span is better. Just as you calculate how successful your business was at the end of the day, and you count in terms of monetary value, similarly at the close of the day, you should check as to what kind of life you have led—whether it was a positive or negative one.

That is the basis of the daily practice. Beside that, you could do some chanting and recitation. If someone has a sufficiently advanced background, one can also engage in tantric practice. However, without proper preparation and foundation, to merely visualize some deity is just mental projection and of no use. This is the process by which we should make our daily life more meaningful.

Normally the practice is categorized into two levels: the practice in the session of meditation and the practice in the postmeditative state. When you are in the session of meditation, you are recharging your batteries. The purpose of regaining your spiritual energy is to enable you to use that energy in your daily life even after the meditation. So the crucial thing is that when you deal with real life, whether you are a teacher, nurse, doctor, politician or in any field, the challenge comes at that moment. That is the real practice. The real test of your practice can be checked by how you live your life and how you deal with your daily affairs. When you engage in your particular individual work, you might frequently encounter certain opportunities to manipulate and deceive other people, and to engage in certain negative acts. Even though you have such an opportunity at your disposal, remind yourself of the need to refrain from such negative acts. The real practice is to refrain from such acts.

Now let us look at the major practice at the time of death. First, once you decide that your practice is to take eons and several lifetimes, that itself gives you a new outlook on death. There are of course many explanations as to why the more subtle mind always remains. There are many reasons for the existence of the subtle mind. As far as the subtle mind is concerned, there is no beginning and no end. Based on texts taught by Nāgārjuna, there are several reasons for this. The grosser level of mind exists due to our brain, and according to the different levels, we can call it the human mind, the animal mind and so on. Those grosser levels of the mind produced by the human brain and human body is what we call the human mind. This mind is dependent on the functioning of the brain. As soon as the brain stops functioning, this mind also stops. But then, using the brain as a cooperative condition, the potential of being able to see the object, the possibility of cultivating the potential to be able to recognize the object should come from a separate cause. This cause is called the substantial cause without which, even though there is the cooperative condition like the brain, it cannot come into existence.

It is because of this that we cannot talk about a particular time and say that this is the first time the subtle mind has come into existence. To accept that would imply that a subtle mind could arise from any other object that is not mind in nature. Therefore, with the view of many lives, it is like changing clothes: you become old and you change.

One's attitude toward death, hence, makes a difference. The clear realization that it is part of one's life and has come into existence due to ignorance and negative emotions makes a difference. From this perspective, the existence of the body is due mainly to attachment. The realization that one's present life is based on ignorance and attachment, and the ability to see one's present existence as something that is projected by ignorance and attachment will also make one realize that something that is a product of ignorance and attachment is bound to cause suffering; that is its nature. Once one is able to gain an insight into this reality, it helps widen one's perspective.

When we talk about the importance of realizing our own existence as a result of ignorance and attachment and something that is suffering in nature, it should be understood within the framework of the Four Noble Truths. This can be understood in two categories or levels—the pure class and the impure class. The impure class means the first two Noble Truths—the true suffering and the origin of suffering. The second level of the Four Noble Truths explains the pure class, the cessation of suffering and the path that leads to this cessation. When we talk about the importance of the realization of suffering, it is extremely important to understand the possibility of achieving the cessation of suffering and removing the causes of such suffering. It is through such an understanding that we will be able to create a strong aspiration to remove suffering. In order to remove suffering, it is extremely important to understand what those sufferings are. If we do not have any understanding about the possibility of removing such suffering, or achieving the state of removing suffering, it is of no use merely contemplating on suffering. It almost sounds like adopting a pessimistic attitude. So it is extremely important to understand the possibility of achieving the higher status, the state of life as a human being or god. There are two kinds of rebirths: one in the more suffering realm and the other in a happier realm.

The same object can be studied from different angles. And because one studies it from different perspectives, one can receive a different impact from the same object. When we talk about the importance of studying the same object from different angles, it is in tune with reality because every single object has several angles and perspectives.

What is the demarcation by which we can determine what is that which exists and that which does not exist? The demarcation between existence and nonexistence is: that which is perceived by a valid perception is existent, and that which is not perceived by a valid perception is nonexistent. This kind of demarcation or explanation is something that would lead you to more questions. It is not easy to understand. Hence, I find Nāgārjuna's definition of the difference between existence and nonexistence both convincing and appropriate.

In his text Nāgārjuna says that a particular phenomenon can be considered existent if its existence is in agreement with the convictions conventionally known by other people, if that kind of acceptance is not contradicted by other valid perceptions and if it is not contradicted by a mind analyzing the ultimate truth.

Thus, this is the only line between something that exists and something that does not. Even in the category of the object that is existing, it could have different aspects or different angles. Here we use the term "relative existence" and from this point of view, everything is relative. There is no absolute existence. Realizing suffering is very helpful when we face some problem or pain. Then our response or attitude is that our very existence involves suffering in nature. This is the base. We take it for granted, and when we encounter it, we do not consider it as something impossible to encounter because we know the reality of our own existence. We have a realistic attitude, and instead of becoming mentally frustrated, we are more eager to develop a negative reaction, and ultimately reach the state where we can completely overcome negative reactions.

At the time of death, the mind encountering death can be of two types: the grosser level of mind and the subtle level of mind. At the grosser level of mind the friends around you at the time of death can help in cultivating certain positive attitudes. But when you enter into the subtle level of mind, your external friends are of no help. It is the kind of positive habituations, whatever you might have in your present life or lives before, that will be taken into account. Hence, from a young age you should get acquainted with death and how to experience the different states of the mental process in the dissolution of the mind. And if possible, make yourself familiar with them through daily meditation and visualization. Instead of fear of death, you may develop an understanding of it. Many years of preparation are needed. Once you have the experience of the deeper and subtle mind through meditation, then finally, when the real opportunity arises, you can actually control the process of death. That, of course, cannot be done by everyone. It can be practiced only by those who have reached a higher level of practice. When this is done in conjunction with the tantric practice, then the practice of transference of consciousness can also be done. But the most important and powerful practice is to remember *bodhicitta*, the infinite altruism. Even though I do different deity yogas in my daily practice, I have more conviction in remembering *bodhicitta* at the time of death. Although I have not fully developed *bodhicitta*, I still feel it has some closeness with death. So at the time of death, concentrate on *bodhicitta* as much as you can.

The practice of *bodhicitta* means cultivating an altruistic mind, wishing to achieve Buddhahood for all suffering sentient beings. It is very, very powerful. If you are able to cultivate this kind of mind even at the level of aspiration, it will definitely leave a strong imprint and impact. With regard to tantric practices, you may practice certain visualizations and the recitation of certain mantras and so forth, but if these tantric practices are not conjoined with other requisite practices, they will often lead to bad results.

In conclusion, practices such as *bodhicitta* automatically bring calmness at the time of death.

From the Buddhist viewpoint, the mind at the time of death is at a very critical stage, and if you are able to leave a strong positive impact at the time of death, that impact will become a very powerful force in continuing a positive experience in the next life. That is for certain. For Buddhist practitioners, that is how you can have a meaningful life and face death. In fact, in the tantric practice, there is a phrase: taking death into the path of "truth body," or dharmakaya. You use the experience of death as a spiritual practice. The intermediary stage after death is also taken into the path of "enjoyment body," or sambhogakaya, and birth is taken into the path of "emanation body," or nirmanakaya.

So the experience we will have at the time of death, whether it will be a positive or negative experience, is very much dependent on how we live our life. The most important thing is that our daily life should be meaningful, positive, and we should live well and happily.

❧

Since the philosophy of Buddhism is not to harm, only to benefit, others, in the case of practical decisions in daily life, if someone wants to kill you and you have no way of escape, what do you do?

From a wider perspective, what is the purpose of your present life? You should also judge your capacity as to how much you can benefit and help others. Of course if someone attacks you, you should escape or avoid the attack. If there is no other possibility, then I think it is your individual right to defend yourself. So without killing, you could perhaps harm the leg or arm of the attacker. That is, if you have the choice.

Are the six realms of samsara actual realms, or are they mere cyclical states of being?
They are a reality. I believe that they actually exist. But at the same time I must say that I am skeptical about the explanations, whether they have to be taken literally or not.

How can one continue to believe in inherent human goodness when one sees the suffering man inflicts on his fellow men?
If you take a wider perspective, all human beings as a people have survived due to the care of their mother or a mother figure for whom they have cared and had compassionate feelings. Without mutual care, compassion and feeling, one cannot survive. The survival of 5.7 billion people is proof of this fact. Another reason is our human

body: negative emotions are very bad for health. Positive emotions or peace of mind are a positive influence on this body. This is the basis of my belief. This does not mean that we have no negative aspects to our nature. Negative emotions are also part of our mind. I think another explanation is that the most effective way to change others' minds is with affection, and not anger. It is very difficult to survive without compassionate feeling. Without anger, not only is survival easier, life itself is much happier. However, without affection, one cannot survive. Therefore, I feel that affection is the dominant force in our life.

Modern science describes a personality determined by genetics and environmental factors. How do you see them compatible with reincarnation?

We call the level of grosser mind the human mind. This level of mind, the grosser level of mind, which is dependent on the human brain or human physical body, is very much related to genetic formation. Here one must understand that modern science is able to provide lots of explanations, and very convincing ones, through these genetic systems. But there are many gray areas—things they have failed to explain—and these are still being investigated.

How can one be sure that what one is doing is in effect positive (that is, which may be negative in everybody's eyes but mine)?

The nature of the very subtle level of the mind or positive factors that are at a very subtle level are natural states of mind. These cannot be explained easily and require detailed explanations or a subtler level of explanation. But generally speaking, all those activities, all those attitudes created by negative emotions, are not meritorious; they are negative. When we talk about the negative afflicted emotions, we are talking about those levels of mind and those attitudes, which when they arise, disturb our peace, leave our whole being completely disturbed and make us uneasy. When hatred, jealousy and extreme kinds of greed develop, at that moment you can never have peace of mind. On the other hand, with strong karuna, or compassion, you may have a feeling of uneasiness when you see others suffering, but you have developed that voluntarily, and with reason. Therefore you accept it and the calmness remains underneath.

All activities and attitudes that are cultivated through negative afflicted emotions are negative deeds. Then there are attitudes that are virtuous motivations or actions because they lead to karma

and to the achievement of a positive higher rebirth.

*I found out this week that my mother has breast cancer.
How does one use a terminal illness as a stepping stone
for personal growth and how can family and friends
make their suffering productive?*

If your mother follows some faith, then think according to her faith. If she is a nonbeliever, then I
think friends need to show a compassionate attitude as far as possible, and share her problems.

*We see that mostly good people suffer, and evil people
keep enjoying benefits and recognition. How then can
one believe in positive daily living?*

In terms of Buddhist philosophy, that kind of ob-
servation is shortsighted. Also this sort of conclusion might have been made in haste. If one makes
a more detailed analysis, one will find that those
troublemakers are definitely not happy. But then,
each individual's future is ultimately his or her
own responsibility. It is better to behave well.
There may be some people whose way of life is
very negative, but this is not something that
should be followed. For example, it is not right to
say that I will kill my parents because someone
else has killed his parents. One should take re-

sponsibility for one's own life, and lead it positively.

This has an explanation from the Buddhist point of view. You might see people who are misbehaving and doing all kinds of negative things. They seem to be enjoying themselves more than the good people. The reason for this is that these people have accumulated few positive deeds, and the amount of their positive deeds is not enough to project them on to a higher, happier existence. They are enjoying their fruit with the few positive deeds they have done, and they are going to quickly run out of the results of their positive deeds.

Why did the human species evolve from lower forms of animals? What is the significance of this?

This is in tune with the general evolutionary process. Buddhists believe that before the galaxies were formed, different energies came together, and solid form and different molecules developed eventually. So the Buddhist explanation and Darwin's theory, as far as evolution is concerned, have many similarities.

How can we help the cause of Tibet? Is there any organization in India supporting the campaign of Tibet?

The government of India and, of course, the state

governments as well as the people of India are very helpful. But then, the Tibet issue is very complicated. The support is, as time goes on, of course, increasing.

Do we have to be born again and again as human beings until we obtain nirvana?
If you are able to achieve nirvana in this life, it is best. If it is not possible, then nirvana can be attained through many successive lives. Attainment of human life is thus necessary.

Don't you think that a certain amount of suffering helps in the spiritual development of the personality?
Provided you are able to transform that calamity or misfortune into the path, encountering suffering definitely contributes to the elevation of the spiritual practice.

By transforming oneself from a negative state of mind to a positive one, how should one tackle the initial stage of doubt and restlessness?
In the initial stage, it is extremely important to have an overview of the whole process of the spiritual path. There may be two kinds of practitioners, with one kind having a good understanding of the different levels of the spiritual path.

This will make a big difference in the cultivation of the practice in their mind and its effectiveness, even though they are practicing on the same subject. That is why, as in the Tibetan tradition, study and meditation are combined. This is a very good tradition.

How does one balance legal rights with moral values?
It seems that law is a separate area, and according to some experts in law, there is no idea of moral values. I don't know. But as a Buddhist practitioner, I believe that in liberal law, individual right and liberty are very, very important. But this does not mean that one should disregard the rights of others or their freedom.

What is your opinion about the recent phenomenon of Ganesh drinking milk, as reported by practitioners worldwide?
I wish to meet a person who has actually witnessed this—a person who has actually fed Ganesh the milk. As a Buddhist, I believe in invisible forces or energies. That is normal. I think in this case, it is better to be skeptical, unless of course it has really happened. It is also possible that it actually happened.

Siri Fort Auditorium, 1995

Path for Spiritual

Practice

Four years have passed since we last met in this hall. Four years mean 1,460 days. Day and night come and go unceasingly without considering whether we utilize them properly or not. They never wait for something good. Not only day and night but our breathing, too, is an ongoing process. In fact, constantly changing nature is the product of the cause of its existence— breath; and this dynamic process of change that we see right across the spectrum of reality is the product of the very cause of creation.

The structure of our body or body particles is also always changing, but essentially we sentient beings are all the same, having the same mind and the same desires. We want more happiness, and want to overcome suffering. There is no difference between a human being and animals or insects as far as desire for happiness and desire to overcome suffering are concerned. However, the difference is that, because of human intelligence and human memory, we can examine the process of suffering from a wider perspective. Philosophy or religion came into existence on that basis.

Because we have a body and mind, we experience pain and pleasure. Pain and pleasure are also largely dependent on our mental attitude. On close examination we notice that physical pain and pleasure can be subdued by the mental condition. Even though the physical state might involve hardship, difficult circumstances or even pain, if our mental state is calm or if we have a proper understanding or the right views, the physical difficulty can be useful. In such cases, although we feel pain, our mental attitude may make us feel happy or quite comfortable. Thus it is possible to overcome suffering and pain with the power of the right mind and attitude.

On the other hand, if the mental state is in pain, then physical discomfort cannot be subdued. Therefore, the mental state is superior. Everybody can train the mind—the transformation of mind can change one's attitude, and broaden one's views or perspective.

There are two levels of spirituality: one is spirituality without religious faith, the other with religious faith. I feel that the first category is very important, because most people, even though they are born into one religion or another, do not pay heed to religious belief in their daily life. People are concerned more about money or material comfort. In that sense, the majority of people in the world today are nonbelievers.

Some of the problems that we are facing today are essentially man-made or products of our own creation; and in that sense there seems to be something lacking in our way of thought or perception. As a result, without any specific intention but due to lack of farsightedness and some carelessness, we allow certain issues to escalate into problems creating dire consequences. Therefore, a particular kind of spirituality without a particular religious faith is both important and relevant. It is wrong to think that concepts of love, compassion and forgiveness are purely religious subjects. It is a narrow understanding that makes us think that these moral issues cannot be practiced without religious faith.

Of course, these issues are covered in all the world's major religions. However, if we think deeply, religious faith and the concepts of love, compassion, kindness and forgiveness are essentially different. According to Buddhism, when a child is born, he or she has no ideology or religious faith. In a way, we can say that at that time the child is free from any ideology or religious faith. But during that time, the child's appreciation of and need for human affection is very strong. Without parental affection the child cannot survive. However, the child can survive without religious faith. In the case of animals, there is obviously no religion, faith or constitution, but they also know how to care for their young. They care, and they also have a sense of altruism. Animals have the capacity to develop limited altruism but, unlike human beings, cannot develop infinite altruism. For example, an animal will lick the wounds of another wounded animal and try to help it. Animals have limited intelligence and also a limited memory, which in comparison to human memory is quite poor. Still, they do have memory. Different animals have different levels of intelligence and some have the intelligence to judge and handle a situation skillfully. Although birds and animals have a certain type of intelligence, human beings have far more intelligence and a greater potential to develop infinite altruism and a powerful memory. Thus, human intelligence and potential to develop altruism are unique to human beings.

Life is a continuous and ever-changing process. Time passes by and nothing ever remains the same. So, we should have a clear awareness of how to utilize time properly and constructively. In order to make life meaningful and purposeful, our wonderful intelligence and unique potential should be tapped to the fullest. It is all right to be a nonbeliever and remain one, yet one should be a warmhearted person and not use one's intelligence destructively. Our intelligence is definitely not meant for destruction. If we create pain for others, ultimately we will suffer—that's only logical. If we give others pleasure, eventually we will get satisfaction. We may get material reward, but it doesn't matter—mentally we will be immensely satisfied. Therefore, in order to live a meaningful and happy life, the unique human features of intelligence, potential of altruism or sense of caring should be utilized constructively. Love, compassion and a sense of forgiveness are, I believe, part of human nature. Faith develops later. With faith one can have a happy life, but without a sense of caring, commitment or responsibility, we cannot be happy or successful.

Everybody needs to take care of his or her health. A happy and calm mind has a very positive influence on one's health. If we are constantly worried and anxious, we ruin our health. Modern medical science is beginning to realize the significance of the mental factor that is crucial for health.

For a happy family, society and community, these inner mental elements are crucial factors.

Sometimes I think that we are far too concerned with action or result without being concerned about the motivation or the causes and conditions of that particular action or event. Sometimes when disasters happen, everyone is in shock, everyone is unhappy. But people don't pay enough attention to the causes and conditions of disasters. Once all the causes and conditions are fully developed, no force can prevent a disaster from happening. It is the law of causality. I think that the inner element or mental element is very important and relevant, especially in today's world. The reality has changed—particularly in this century. This is due to technology, information, a deeper awareness about the reality, population and man-made problems such as pollution and other factors. People who live in Delhi are now experiencing the consequences of the "good work" or perhaps carelessness of the previous decades.

Despite the changes, it seems that our perceptions and attitudes are lagging behind the times. In today's world and reality, the demarcation between nations and the distance between continents no longer have much relevance. The whole planet is very small. When you look at Earth from outer space, the image we get is that of a tiny sphere and this, in fact, is Earth's status. It is important for us to accept this so that we can change our way of thinking.

In this country, one's existence is closely related to the existence of other people. Economy, education and many other fields are heavily interdependent. The concepts of "us" and "them" are no longer relevant. The whole world is like a part of your body. Take, for example, my foot and hand. If there is some pain in my leg, my hand goes there to rub it and nurture it. Similarly, your neighbor may have a serious problem; but he is still your neighbor and a part of your community. You have to develop a sense of compassion, caring, and a sense of connectedness because the destruction of your neighbor, or your neighboring country, is actually a destruction of yourself. Under these circumstances we need a broader view to look at humanity as one human family. Yes, there are different races, different customs, religions—if you want to look for differences, they can always be found. In spite of that, we share the same small planet, and if others suffer, we suffer eventually. If we are happy, they are also going to benefit. So in this respect we need a sense of global responsibility, a universal responsibility.

If one thinks more about others, then a sense of caring develops. This way of thinking brings more inner strength. Caring for others makes one feel that others are okay. On the other hand, if one thinks only about oneself, it perpetuates a feeling of inadequacy within oneself. Still there is the feeling that one needs more, and this kind of feeling automatically brings suspicion, resulting in more anxiety and restlessness. The same mind, with the same concerns of pain and suffering, is concerned only with one's own pain and happiness. This creates an emptiness and the result is fear and insecurity. But the same attitude with the concern for others with pain and suffering brings inner strength. Worrying about oneself brings more fear, more doubt. And doubt and suspicion are always accompanied with a sense of insecurity and loneliness.

If we are to be selfish, we should be wisely selfish. If we think about ourselves all the time, it will eventually bring more suffering. So we should think about others for our own benefit. If we analyze our daily life and also observe our neighbors', we ultimately develop some kind of conviction. Altruism thus benefits others and also brings immense benefit to oneself.

Every human being, whether educated or uneducated, rich or poor or physically deformed, has the potential to develop some of these basic human qualities. From birth we all have the potential to develop these good qualities and human values. Therefore, we have to make every effort to increase and sustain them with confidence. On the other hand, hatred and too much suspicion have no value, nor can they bring about a good result. Hatred or ill-feeling toward one's neighbors will not harm them or make them distrustful, but hatred or ill-feeling will directly harm one's own peace of mind. For example, if one has a problem with one's neighbor, and wants the neighbor to suffer in a similar manner, that objective cannot be achieved or the desire fulfilled. On the contrary, if one has negative feelings toward one's neighbor, it will eventually destroy one's digestion and mind and make one extremely unhappy. One's children, wife or husband will end up suffering.

In my experience, the calmer you are, the more you think about and practice altruism and other good things, the more you benefit. This mental state, these qualities, are very relevant and useful for a happy and successful life. By thinking along these lines, you will eventually be convinced that anger and hatred are very bad for your life and health. A compassionate attitude and a sense of caring are good not only for your peace of mind but also very good for your health. Once we develop a clear awareness about the positive and negative aspects of these different thoughts, this in itself affects our attitude, bringing about the transformation of our mind. This is one level of spirituality. Be a warmhearted person, a good person. Regardless of whether it has meaning, our very existence is a reality. It is very important to utilize our existence for constructive purposes.

At the second level, to the believers, I want to say what I have emphasized many times in the past—that once you accept a religious faith, you should implement its teaching as much as you can. In other words, the teachings or that faith should be part of your daily life. If you implement them, then as time goes by, year by year, a kind of gradual transformation will occur and you will get real benefit. By merely reciting a prayer or some mantras, you will not create much of an effect. It is customary for Buddhists and Hindus to make a daily offering in front of an idol such as Ganesh, Buddha, Tara or Shiva. An offering of fruit, flowers or incense is made and the name of the god repeated without much meditation. Similarly, a mere mantra or prayer will not have much effect.

Unfortunately, many followers or believers perform a daily *puja* and nothing more. This is not sufficient. We need to go deep inside our mind or consciousness. Without that, our view, our life or our way of thinking can't change.

If we accept a particular religion, we should be very serious and practice it. Then, eventually, there will be real change. This is very important. Take, for instance, the Tibetan community. The majority of people are Buddhist, but their manner of practice is very inadequate due to the lack of awareness or knowledge about Buddha dharma. Many Indians are also in the same boat.

Many of the texts that have been translated from Sanskrit sources into Tibetan are Buddhist texts. In these Buddhist texts there are references to and citations from many philosophical texts that belong to the non-Buddhist traditions of ancient India. So there are explanations of the concept of moksha and how to achieve this goal through meditation, samadhi and *vipassana*.

In the last thirty-eight years spent in India, I have had many meetings with religious masters and philosophers. Except for a few, they all seem to say that after you accept your religious tradition, the next step is to study, then follow it up by its implementation, which is very essential. For the study, one should not be content to merely recite some mantra or prayer and keep a rosary. The great meditators meditate without any rosary. They simply watch their mind, analyze phenomena and think deeply. That is the proper way. Even in the scriptures that mention yoga tantra or deity yogas, the main practice is meditation. When one gets tired, one can recite mantras. People usually recite them without doing any meditation. Not only is this wrong, it is insufficient.

Once you adopt or accept a religion, you should be very sincere and very serious. However, if you are too serious and narrow-minded, there is the danger of becoming what one calls a fundamentalist. If religion is not properly practiced, then there is a danger of believing only in one's own religion and dismissing the others, thus becoming fundamentalist.

I want to share my views about the harmony of different religious traditions. I am a Buddhist; and sometimes I describe myself as a staunch Buddhist because, to me, the practice of Buddhism is the best, and Buddhist explanations are very logical. I truly believe that for me Buddhism is the best, but it is certainly not the best for everyone. People with different mental dispositions need different religions. One religion simply cannot satisfy everyone. Therefore, for the individual, the concept of one religion and one truth is very important. Without this, one cannot develop genuine faith and follow it faithfully.

With regard to the community, we obviously need the concept of several religions and several truths—pluralism. This is both necessary and relevant. This is the way to overcome contradictions between several religions and several truths and one religion and one truth. Thus, I believe that one has one religion and one truth on the individual level, and one has several religions and several truths on the community level. Otherwise it is difficult to solve this problem.

It is hypocrisy to say that all religions are the same. Different religions have different views and fundamental differences. But it does not matter, as all religions are meant to help in bringing about a better world with better and happier human beings. On this level, I think that through different philosophical explanations and approaches, all religions have the same goal and the same potential. Take the concept of the creator and self-creation for instance. There are big differences between the two, but I feel they have the same purpose. To some people, the concept of the creator is very powerful in inspiring the development of self-discipline, becoming a good person with a sense of love, forgiveness and devotion to the ultimate truth—the Creator or God.

The other concept is self-creation: if one wants to be good, then it is one's own responsibility to be so. Without one's own efforts one cannot expect something good to come about. One's future is entirely dependent on oneself: it is self-created. This concept is very powerful in encouraging an individual to be a good and honest person. So you see, the two are different approaches but have the same goal.

Many of you know the Four Noble Truths, the famous teachings of Buddha. This is the foundation of Buddha dharma. Unfortunately, many Buddhists believe that Mahayana, Hinayana and Vajrayana, the three *yanas* are incompatible. This is not true.

During the thirties, forties and fifties, some Western scholars described Tibetan Buddhism as Lamaism, implying that Tibetan Buddhism is not pure Buddhism—that it is somehow polluted. The Hinayana or Theravada tradition is the foundation of Buddha dharma. The Four Noble Truths, the Thirty-seven Aspects of the path to Enlightenment, the three higher trainings (trainings in morality, concentration and wisdom or insight), are the essence and foundation of Theravada or Hinayana teaching. Without this, how can one practice Mahayana?

Sometimes, those who follow the Mahayana tradition feel that they have the greater vehicle and look down on Hinayana teaching. I think that is very wrong. On the other hand, some people of the Hinayana tradition feel that the Mahayana school of thought is polluted, and not part of the true Buddhist tradition. I think that is also very wrong. Without the Mahayana teaching, it is very difficult to understand nirvana or moksha. Without understanding emptiness—the concept of *shunya*—it is very, very difficult to understand the possibility or the concept of nirvana. Of course, one can say that since Buddha stated that there is nirvana and achieved it himself, there must be nirvana. This sort of blind faith is all right; but it is only through repeated analytical meditation, and by examining the function and nature of the mind, the reality of phenomena and the nature of negative emotion, that one can eventually develop a sense of moksha or nirvana.

Without the detailed explanations of the six great masters of India—Nagarjuna, Aryadeva, the two supreme masters of Vinaya and others—it is difficult to understand the concept of nirvana or *nirodha*. All these masters are Mahayana teachers and monks. They practice the teaching of Hinayana, implement Vinaya practice, remain good bhikshus and propagate Mahayana teachings.

Some people believe that Hinayana, Mahayana and Tantrayana are a sort of historical or chronological development; but as a Buddhist, I do not agree with this. If we want a conventional understanding of the evolution of these teachings, it is possible to develop a historical reading of the different *yanas.*

Mahayana teaching is a wonderful Buddhist tradition, but without the practice of the basic Buddhist teaching of Hinayana, one can't be a genuine Buddhist. So, one needs to practice the Hinayana doctrine as a foundation and then practice the teachings of the Mahayana sutra, namely, that of infinite altruism which is developed step by step through certain techniques. Similarly, Vajrayana uses Hinayana as a foundation, Mahayana Sutrayana as a secondary addition, and Vajrayana as the third component. That is the way of the true Vajrayana practitioner. Without the two previous *yanas,* Tantrayana would be a mere name. The use of impressive costumes, ritual implements and mantras does not characterize the true Vajrayana practitioner. Of course, some exceptions exist, but, generally speaking, this is the basic line of Buddha dharma. And when we refer to it, it is very important to go according to the basic line.

As I mentioned before, referring to Tibetan Buddhism as Lamaism is wrong because it was not invented by the Tibetan lamas. Whenever we come across an important point, we always quote a reliable Indian master. This method of authentication of a particular point or issue by citing Indian texts as an ultimate authority was so widely accepted that, in some cases, certain views are refuted on the grounds that they have no basis in any authentic Indian text.

A Tibetan master explained the text of one of the Indian masters who mentioned Tibet as the Land of the Snow because of the whiteness of the mountains there. However, without the light of Indian masters, Tibet still remains dark and blind despite the whiteness of the snow. Thus, these great Indian masters are truly the openers of the Tibetan mind.

The Tibetan commentators seem to have developed a very sophisticated hermeneutic tradition to be able to understand and read these classical Indian texts, so that whenever a classical Indian text is being commented upon, there is a comparative approach that brings together the various points at issue and discussions from different angles to hammer a single point home. The multifaceted hermeneutic approach in the Tibetan tradition of commentary is apparent. All these Tibetan masters made a great contribution.

However, the basis of all these great works was cultivated by the Indian masters. I always consider them as our teachers. So the concept that Tibetan Buddhism is Lamaism is not correct. Tibetan Buddhism is actually the genuine teachings of the Buddha that were probably combined at different periods till they finally reached Tibet as one body of text. Tibetan Buddhism is therefore the complete form of Buddha dharma.

I usually describe the essence of Buddha dharma in two sentences: If you can, help others, serve others. If you cannot, at least refrain from harming others. The basic theme of Theravada teaching is self-liberation. Of course, karuna, or compassion, is also involved, though it is not compulsory. The main aim is self-liberation while serving others as much as one can. The essence is: don't harm others. In Mahayana, the emphasis is on altruism or *bodhicitta,* the desire to achieve Buddhahood in order to serve or help other sentient beings. That kind of Buddha mind is the main message or main practice. So, *mahakaruna,* or the greater compassion, is compulsory. This is the basic cause of altruism. It does not matter what happens to you; one needs to help and serve others.

In order to help others or refrain from harming others, there need to be reasons. Without a reason it is meaningless. There should be a reason as to why we need the practice of ahimsa, or nonviolence, and why we need to serve others or refrain from harming them. The rationale for engaging in a way of life of nonviolence, refraining from harming others or engaging in altruism is the appreciation of the interdependent nature of reality.

Buddhist teachings refer to three different levels or meanings of interdependence. One is understanding the phenomenon of interdependence in terms of causes and conditions; so dependence here is in the sense of causal dependence. The second is dependence in terms of the concept of parts and whole, in the sense that every phenomenon is composed of its constituent parts. And the third level is the way in which we understand the relationship and basis of designation.

Our pains and pleasures are related to their own causes and conditions. Because we want happiness and do not want to suffer, we have to take care of the causes and conditions of our pain and pleasure. By helping others, and by giving, we experience more pleasure, which results in more comfort. If we cause others pain, the result will be that we will suffer.

Our happy experiences are not the result of just one factor, but depend on many factors. Therefore, we have to take care of all these different factors. When we have a deeper understanding of the Buddhist teachings of interdependence—that even a single event has multiple causes and conditions that contribute to that event—then we will really have a deep philosophical basis for the ecological perspective— respect for the natural laws of the environment. The concept of interdependence helps to widen our perspective. It automatically makes us aware of the importance of causality-relations, which in turn brings forth a more holistic view.

Ahimsa, or nonviolence, is not just not harming others, it is an act of compassion. The theory of interdependence is a very important one as it widens our perspective. It is on the basis of the interpretation of the Buddha's teachings on interdependence that different philosophical schools evolved in India. A quantum mechanical understanding of the physical universe seems to be pointing toward some kind of relationship between the observer and the observed, and how the thought processes of the observer seem to make an impact on the observed phenomenon, which again resonates the Madhyamika discourse on the nature of reality.

Given that, through the Madhyamika analytical process or philosophical examination, we arrive at a point where we feel there is a need to appreciate the disparity between appearance and reality. Madhyamika speaks of phenomena as being an illusion. Therefore, according to Madhyamika, all phenomena are devoid of true existence and substantial reality. However, there are differences between the various Indian interpreters or scholars when they try to understand this great insight of Nāgārjuna.

Nāgārjuna is seen by the Tibetan tradition as the founder of the Madhyamika school of middle way philosophy. Aryadeva, the principal disciple of Nāgārjuna, was the successor of the Nāgārjuna lineage of teachings. Arya Asanga is seen by the Tibetan tradition as the founder of the Cittamatra or mind-only school of Indian philosophy, and Vasubhandu was his successor and the great upholder of the mind-only school of Indian Buddhism.

What is common to both these great Mahayana schools of Indian Buddhism—the middle way school of Madhyamika and the mind-only school of Cittamatra—is the acceptance or recognition of the cardinal importance of the Mahayana scriptures and the Prajnaparamita ("Perfection of Wisdom") Sutras in particular. When the Madhyamikas interpret such expressions and statements in the Paramitayana, where the Buddha is reported to have stated that all phenomena are devoid of self-nature or an intrinsic being, it is understood in terms of the interdependent nature of reality. In a way, interdependent nature of reality is used as a reason to infer this absence of independent existence or self-nature. In other words, they present the paramita sutras—the teachings on emptiness—in terms of interdependent origination or interdependence.

According to the Tibetan tradition, Nāgārjuna is believed to have come four hundred years after the Buddha, and Arya Asanga about nine hundred years after the death of the Buddha. Arya Asanga is referred to in some sutras as a highly realized being, having attained the third *bhoomi,* or the third bodhisattva level of spiritual realization. According to Tibetan tradition, Arya Asanga is believed to be the upholder of Nāgārjuna's Madhyamika tradition, and the reason for his initiating this new lineage of Mahayana Buddhism is that in Nāgārjuna's interpretation of the Prajnaparamita Sutras, he appreciated that there is a potential for some people to fall into some sort of nihilistic understanding of the Mahayana sutras. Therefore, instead of accepting the statement that all phenomena are devoid of an intrinsic being, Arya Asanga developed a new interpretation that allowed the practitioners to approach the Mahayana scriptures and still accept the validity of the Buddha's teaching that all phenomena are devoid of an intrinsic being. The way this is interpreted is that the absence of intrinsic being is understood differently in different contexts—in the sense that all dependent phenomena are said to be devoid of an independent process of production, and all imputed and thoroughly established phenomena are said to be devoid of an intrinsic reality. The point is that Arya Asanga developed an interpretation of the Mahayana scriptures that was different from Nāgārjuna's understanding of it.

Arya Asanga interpreted the Buddha's statement that all phenomena are devoid of an intrinsic being in terms of what is known as the theory of three natures—that all phenomena possess three natures: the dependent nature, the imputed nature and the consummated nature. He explained these three natures as having different senses of being devoid of intrinsic being. Arya Asanga not only developed this new approach to understanding the Mahayana scriptures, but also grounded his interpretation in the Buddha's own words. For example, in the Mahayana scripture known as the Samdhinirmochana Sutra, the sutra unraveling the thought of the Buddha is used as the principal text to substantiate the authenticity and validity of Arya Asanga's interpretation of the Mahayana scriptures.

In this three-natured theory, the second is the imputed nature, and the absence of the intrinsic being is understood in terms of the imputed nature being devoid of any self-defining characteristics. Imputed nature can generally be spoken of as being of two kinds. There can be certain types of imputation that are mere fantasies and have no basis in reality, and there are other types of imputation that can be a form of labels but have some bearing on reality.

The first nature is the dependent nature; and its very idea suggests that phenomena or events come into being as a result of the forces of other factors. So this dependent nature is not of independent production. Arya Asanga's interpretation suggests that it is the imputed phenomenon that lacks self-defining characteristics; but dependent nature and consummated nature do possess some degree of self-defining characteristics or intrinsic nature. This interpretation of the Prajnaparamita Sutras, which is exemplified by the Cittamatras, leads the practitioner or the thinker to such depths of his or her analysis in understanding the nature of reality that at a certain point the person begins to lose the concreteness of the external world. Therefore, the Cittamatras came to the conclusion that the external world that we perceive is an illusion and it lacks the concreteness that we project. So the external or material world, the physical realm, is, in the ultimate sense, nothing but an extension of one's mind—a projection—that is ultimately led to the position where its concreteness and reality are denied. It becomes very important for that school to understand how the perception of the external world arises. If the external world that we perceive is a mere illusion, how does one begin to perceive the concreteness or reality of the external world? Here it becomes crucial for the school to provide an explanation for this process, and therefore, in Cittamatra discourse, we find a lot of discussion on the function and the nature of mind, particularly on how perceptions arise. There are discussions on how the perception of the external world arises as a result of activation of different imprints upon a particular kind of consciousness that they label as "foundational consciousness," or *alayavijana*. So the Cittamatra

school not only discusses the six types of consciousness—the five sensory faculties in addition
to the mental faculty—but also discusses the fundamental consciousness or fundamental stored
consciousness.

Given that, it becomes important for that school
to understand how the process of perception begins and how the fundamental stored consciousness is the repository of many of the imprints that
have been stored as a result of our cognitive and
emotional experiences. It becomes important to
give an account of what sort of imprints are left on
the stored consciousness. The Cittamatras refer to a
particular kind of imprint that they label the imprint of sameness. This imprint is supposed to explain how successive instances of perception of the
material world arise. For example, if we perceive a
blue object, that perception can continue up to a
certain point so that the successive instances of the
blue object are said to be resulting from the activation of imprints stored in the consciousness.

The Cittamatra school classifies different types
of imprints as imprints of language and habit formation; and it is on this basis that they explain
why when we perceive a blue object we have the
concept of blueness; or why the label "blue" has
an intrinsic relationship with the object; and this

kind of perception is said to arise as a result of successive experiences we have of using the language of blueness. Thus, the language imprints and habit formation result in this kind of perception.

The Cittamatras speak of a third type of imprint that is said to be formed by our habit of clinging to or grasping at something concrete. It is because of this that when we perceive a blue object, not only do we perceive something blue but we also perceive an intimate relationship between our perception of blue and the blue object we see. We feel that there is something objectively real about that blue object that justifies the usage of the term. In reality, the language, and the term that we use to describe that object, is in some sense arbitrary; it is a label, a symbol. But this is not how we feel when we are confronted with a blue object. When we are confronted with a blue object, we get an instinctive sense that it is really blue and something objectively real about it forces us to use the language of blueness. This kind of misperception is said to be the result of what the Cittamatras call habits and imprints formed by our long habituation for clinging and objectivity.

So, in reality, that blue objectively does not

have any reason or ground for being the referent for the term "blue"; and this relationship between the symbol and the signified is in some sense arbitrary. Therefore, the Cittamatras call that relationship a mere convention. It is on this basis that they argue that the imputation of blueness to that object lacks any objective and substantial reality. But this is not to say that imputation does not exist. The belief that the blue object is objectively real and also in some ultimate sense the true referent of the term "blue" and the concept of blueness is pure fantasy. It is this belief that is the key focus of refutation by the Cittamatra school. So the Cittamatras argue that the fact that we have this misperception is very evident, because if someone asks us what is a blue object, we would point to a blue object and say, "That is blue." This indicates that in our normal understanding of the world, we do not deal with the world as if the term "blue" or the concept "blueness" is a mere label or symbol; rather, we act as if it has some kind of intrinsic value, some ultimate relationship between the object and the term or the label. This method of understanding is an illusion; and the Cittamatras argue that clinging to that kind of belief is at the root of our confusion concerning the nature of reality and the awareness and insight, that this is false, and that these terms and labels do not relate to the object in an objective sense. This method of understanding constitutes true insight to the ultimate nature of reality and it is in these terms that the Cittamatras explain and understand the Mahayana teachings on emptiness.

Therefore, we find in the Mahayana scriptures and commentaries that the Cittamatras or the mind-only philosophers approach the world and engage with reality in what is known as the Four Quests. One is a quest for labels or terms, seeking a true reference. The next is the quest for the meaning of the terms and concepts; the third is the quest for the nature or being of the phenomenon; and the fourth is the quest for the self-defining characteristics of the phenomenon. It is through inquiry into these four different dimensions of phenomena that the Cittamatras arrive at their understanding of the true view, which they describe as the mere consciousness, or mind-only.

In conclusion, according to the Mahayana sutra, the concept of *shunya* carries the most important tool—one according to Cittamatra and one according to Madhyamika. These two different concepts of *shunya* are considered very, very important and also very complicated. The whole

Vajrayana teaching is based on understanding of the *shunya* theory and it is crucial to have some experience or understanding of it, either according to the Cittamatra or the Madhyamika. Of course, if we analyze various points of view, we find that the Madhyamika concept is preferred. Without the concept of *shunya,* it is very difficult, and useless, to have deity yoga or to try to visualize oneself as a deity. Therefore, to practice Vajrayana, you have to practice *bodhicitta* and have some understanding of *shunya.* On the basis of their combination, the deity then becomes very powerful, and very effective.

꒛

How can nirvana and samsara be of the same state?
Here, if one has developed a deeper understanding of the teachings on nonsubstantiality of all phenomena, then of course one would have arrived at an understanding not only of nirvana and samsara, but the idea that all phenomena possess sameness in the ultimate sense. They are all nonsubstantial; they are all devoid of intrinsic reality. So, from this point of view, of course, as Nāgārjuna states, if one understands the true nature of samsara, one will also have true insight into nirvana, and vice versa. Therefore, one must

not impose a false reading on Nāgārjuna's statement, thinking that in fact Nāgārjuna might be
saying that this samsara—the state of unenlight-
ened existence that we are in—is, in reality, the
same as nirvana, the enlightened state.

*How do we know that there is a soul and that man is re-
born according to karma?*
From the Buddhist point of view, the theory of
rebirth is not explained in terms of the concept
of karma. The theory of rebirth should be understood on the basis of our understanding of the
nature of causality, because according to Buddhism every event must have preceding causes
and conditions. Therefore, even a single cognitive event—say, an instance of consciousness or
mind—must have causes and conditions; and so
through this process we can trace the beginningless continuum to the consciousness. And once
we are able to develop that kind of understanding
of the causal process, then the theory of rebirth
develops naturally on the basis of that kind of
causal understanding.

Now where does karma fit in relation to the
theory of rebirth? It determines the kind of rebirth an individual may have. Good karma results
in a favorable rebirth, and negative karma results

in an unfavorable one. Of course, we must understand that when we are talking of karma we are talking about an instance of the causal process; karma is part of that process. When we speak of karma we are referring not just to an event but rather an event that involves an agent, a doer, an act. Karma is an act committed by an agent, a being with motivation, determining the cause of that process.

After arguing with someone, how do you overcome the feeling that you are right and the other person is wrong? How do you get over ill-feelings toward another when that person has maliciously wronged you?

As to the second part of the question I would recommend that you read the chapter on patience in Shantideva's *Bodhisattva Charya Avatara: A Guide to the Bodhisattva's Way of Life*.

However, I would like to point out that when talking about cultivating patience and tolerance against someone who has harmed us for no reason, we are not talking about giving in to the wrongs being done upon us, nor are we talking about endorsing the other person's actions. It is important to understand that patience does not mean mere giving in or meekness; rather, patience is a deliberate stand one adopts on the basis that you deliberately resolve not to retaliate against the harm done by the other person. It is an active state rather than a state of meekness, and in some instances, certain actions and wrongs done by others may require strong countermeasures. But even these measures can be adopted on the basis of patience and tolerance. Once you begin to realize the multiplicity of standpoints and perspectives and the complexity of the issues, then there is no need to cling to one's own standpoint thinking that that is the truth.

Of course there may be instances where the two parties have diametrically opposed positions or viewpoints. For example, the dispute between the mind-only school and the middle way (Madhyamika) philosophers in terms of their interpretation of the ultimate nature of phenomena. What is at issue is whether all phenomena are devoid of intrinsic being or whether some phenomena do possess an intrinsic being. Of course, here the Cittamatras take one viewpoint while Madhyamikas take another, and, in some sense, these two viewpoints are diametrically opposed. In such instances, one can look at the dispute from the point of view of the purposes that the two different viewpoints serve: how one viewpoint serves the philosophical inclination of some people, and the other serves the philosophical inclination as well as the quest of other people. Then the fact that they have different purposes, and this appreciation of the diversity of purpose, can reduce the clinging to one's own position.

How should we balance environmental protection with the needs of humans, such as deforestation, which causes the death of many organisms but without which people would die?

Conflicts and contradictions are in some sense what makes us human beings. On the practical level this issue is a complicated one. In India, for example, the economic situation is very poor and very difficult, especially in the rural areas and in the Himalayan range where people depend very much on the forest for their livelihood. So, unless we show them an alternative, it is difficult to stop these things. We have to make progress in a broader perspective because so many things are interrelated. For instance, family planning is also very important, so I think the holistic approach is necessary.

I would like to know how Mahayana and Hinayana help a student.

For a Buddhist student it is necessary to study these teachings and implement them step by step. The Tibetan tradition clearly practices this as we both study and implement the teachings. Even though some may not implement it immediately, the entire plan should be made very clear: this practice is for today, this practice comes later, and so on, so that we have the complete process in mind.

In my society it is expected that I measure my success in material terms. If instead I measure my success in terms of compassion and inner peace, I am considered a fool. How can I find the patience and self-discipline to overcome the frustration and doubt that this causes?

Society does have the habit of judging people's success in terms of material success, but I would like to point out here that just because a conventional perspective like this exists, it does not mean that it is valid, because we know from our own personal experience that at this point in history we, the members of this generation, are suffering the negative consequences of many of the so-called conventional wisdoms of the past generations.

Recently, I had the pleasure of participating in a major conference in America that concentrated on dealing with and overcoming various social problems that particularly an affluent society is confronted with today. The participants of this conference were from various social organizations in the health care and social welfare fields. The consensus was that one of the principal causes of these social problems is the lack or inadequate amount of compassion and sense of caring in the community. So, it is my belief and conviction that as a result of all these experiences and the insights gained by people from different walks of life, it will gradually dawn on us that it is critical to cultivate an appreciation of the value of many of the inner qualities of human beings in society.

What makes His Holiness most happy?
Sound sleep and good food!

Pay attention not only to the cultivation of knowledge but to the cultivation of qualities of the heart, so that at the end of education, not only will you be knowledgeable, but you will also be a warmhearted and compassionate person.

Modern School, Barakhamba, 1997

The Two
Truths

The first half of my lecture will be the academic explanation of the meaning of truth and the other half will be about how to implement it in today's life on the basis of the whole philosophy and system of truth.

The bottom line is that we are all human beings who want happiness and do not want suffering. On that basis we are trying to investigate the nature of external and internal truth. There are different kinds of philosophies and systems of teaching in human society, and Buddhism is one of them. We have so many different philosophies that one philosophy simply cannot satisfy all humankind; this is why we have so many different teachings of spiritual systems today. It is very important to have various teaching systems for all sorts of people.

As a follower of Buddha, I have learned a few things. But I am still learning and gaining knowledge. I am not an expert but a Buddhist monk who is sincerely trying to follow his faith in his daily life. Especially when I face a problem, this teaching is very useful in maintaining my mental stability. These teachings give me flexibility and inner strength. So whenever someone asks me to explain these philosophies or teachings, I regard it my responsibility and duty to try to do so.

The basic foundation of Buddhist philosophy is made up of two truths: if you find something useful in these teachings, you should investigate it for yourself and try to implement it in your daily life; if you find nothing important, then you should just leave it. Most of you know about the Four Noble Truths (true suffering, true cause of suffering, true cessation and true path). They are the foundation of Buddhism. The goal of every sentient being is happiness—permanent happiness. It is both wonderful and worthwhile if permanent happiness can be achieved. That means no more suffering, lasting peace and satisfaction. Usually after a moment of happiness and pleasure, some problem or the other arises. That kind of pleasure is not permanent. Hence, these Four Noble Truths become significant. Because we do not want suffering, it is most important to investigate the causes of suffering. Is it possible to eliminate them? If so, it is worth the attempt.

Otherwise, there is no point in trying. The third Noble Truth is the truth of cessation (what we call nirvana or moksha). If it is indeed possible to achieve cessation of the causes of suffering, then it is fruitful to find out ways and means to purify one's own mind or to eliminate the causes of suffering. That is the fourth Truth.

It also indicates the law of cause and effect and interdependency, and is the basis of *shunya*. The theory of *shunya* is based on the idea that things are interdependent. For every thing has different aspects, and if you compare these aspects you find that all things are related. Its very nature is relative, and emptiness refers to its ultimate nature. Thus there is the possibility to create new things, and these will change since things depend upon other factors. If things exist absolutely and by themselves, then there is no way you can make new efforts in order to achieve a new experience or new goal. If things are absolute, there is no way to effect changes by any means. This is the essence of the two truths.

There is also the turning of the three wheels of the doctrine. In the first wheel, Buddha taught the Four Noble Truths. For people more disciplined and purified in their conduct, he taught the Wisdom-Perfection Sutra. It contains mainly the teaching of emptiness. However, depending upon the way people interpreted the thought behind that teaching, the two tenets—the Cittamatra and the Madhyamika—came into being.

In the last turning of wheel of the doctrine, Buddha mainly emphasized how to purify the delusions of the mind. In other words, the mind has clarity that can be used to develop it in a holistic way. The Four Noble Truths were taught along with their sixteen aspects. The characteristics of the aspect of true suffering are impermanence, suffering, emptiness and selflessness. In general, there is the teaching of the Four Seals and this teaching is commonly accepted by all Buddhists. The Four Seals are: all conditioned things are impermanent; all contaminated things are suffering; phenomena are selfless and empty; nirvana is peace.

On the subject of the selflessness of phenomena, the four different tenets came into existence depending upon the differences of the view. They are Vaibhashika, Sautantrika, Cittamatra and Madhyamika. All these make a presentation of the Two Truths. But Vaibhashika and Sautantrika accept the Two Truths as being different entities.

According to the Vaibhashika, the conventional truth means any phenomenon that cannot hold its identity after disintegration. Whereas even after splitting into parts mentally or when disintegrated physically, if the phenomenon can hold its identity, then that is the ultimate truth. For example, the microphone is a conventional truth, and if we split the different parts that constitute its existence, its very entity is lost. But when we come to the very subtle nature of this particular instrument, we cannot split it or throw out its core. This specific nature is referred to as "ultimate." According to this system, it accepts the partless particle and as far as consciousness is concerned, it accepts the consciousness as momentarily partless.

According to the Sautantrika tenet, conventional truth is the one that cannot ultimately function, whereas ultimate truth is the one that can. For instance, a flower is the ultimate truth according to this system because a flower is itself produced by causes and conditions and it can also produce effect. Therefore, if it is able to produce effect, it is called functional.

Since this particular object—the flower—is not anything other than the flower, it has all the reverse qualities of not being other phenomena. Thus, that particular quality is merely a mental interpretation, and this interpretation of the quality of that flower is what is called the conventional truth. According to both the mind-only and the Madhyamika systems, the Two Truths have the same entity but are different. They say that even if they are of a different entity, if you familiarize your mind with the conventional and the ultimate truth of any particular object, it will not be able to harm the object of negation that is true grasping or self-grasping, because the subject and its nature are of a different entity. Therefore, the different entity of the subject and the object is not acceptable.

Even though the entity of the conventional truth and the ultimate truth is the same, the Two Truths are different. If they were the same, then it would amount to saying that if one realizes and understands a particular phenomenon like a pot correctly, then the ultimate truth or the emptiness of the pot would also be realized directly. If we follow the system propounded in the Cittamatra school, it undoubtedly explains the presentation of these two truths in nature, but according to the Madhyamika tenet, this explanation is not so perfect as it does not establish the qualities of the self as empty.

According to the Madhyamika school, every subject or phenomenon has two qualities: its conventional quality and its ultimate quality. In other words, it has a temporary quality and a lasting, real or permanent one. These two qualities are inevitably present in one object, and have some entity. When exponents of the mind-only or Cittamatra school explain the Two Truths, they start by explaining the three characteristics or signs and base their explanation of the Two Truths on that.

The purpose of explaining the Two Truths is that we are basically confused and ignorant about reality. In order to identify that ignorance and eradicate that confusion, one has to know the real nature of phenomena. Thus, the Two Truths play an important role in understanding reality.

According to the mind-only school, all phenomena can be categorized into three types: dependent phenomena, imputed phenomena and thoroughly established phenomena. The dependent phenomenon becomes the basis of designation, and it is based on this dependent phenomenon because of conceptuality and the imprint that has been left on one's mind from beginningless time. One gets the tendency of grasping phenomena as externally and substantially existent and external to the mind. But this way of looking at phenomena is wrong. They actually have the nature of nonexistence. In other words, the phenomenon that appears external to us is of the same substance as the mind itself. The subject mind and the object realized by the mind are of the same substance. If we grasp and apprehend the mind and the object as being made of different substances, it is wrong. It is the object of negation; there is no such existence. Such an existence is empty. Emptiness here signifies lack of substantial separateness of the mind and the object. Therefore, this quality of lack of substantial separateness of the mind and the object characterizes the quality of the basis of designation of the dependent phenomenon.

In other words, according to this school, the ultimate truth is something that is the ultimate object of the mind, and a purified object. Believers of this tenet do not accept the existence of an external object that is substantially different from the mind. To the mind, all phenomena, all appearing phenomena, are of the same nature. There is also a second school, Svatantrika Madhyamika, that accepts the theory of the mind-only school. But then the *Prasangika-Madhyamika* philosophers reject this view. The prominent followers of the Madhyamika refute the presentation of the mind-only school saying that if you do not accept the existence of the external phenomena, you cannot accept the existence of the mind as well. The Cittamatra school says that the external object that is substantially separate from the mind is nonexistent, and that if you try to analyze the external object through parts, it cannot be found. Therefore, the external phenomena are nonexistent. In response, the Madhyamika school says that if you are unable to find an external object when you analyze it through parts, it does not signify the nonexistence of this phenomenon; it signifies the noninherent existence of it. If you say that external phenomena are nonexistent, then you have to accept the mind as nonexistent as well. Thus, propounders of the Madhyamika tenet accept the existence of the mind as well as of external phenomena.

According to the Madhyamika school, there are two ways of explaining the Two Truths: one based on the existence of conceptual mind and the other based on the existence of the non-conceptual mind. But if we were to provide an explanation that was acceptable to both the conceptual and the nonconceptual minds, it would be something like this: conventional truth is that phenomenon that is found by a conventional mind, whereas the ultimate truth is that phenomenon that is found by an ultimate mind analyzing the nature of the ultimate phenomenon. This is the explanation as given in Chandrakirti's *Madhyamika-Avatara.*

According to the *Bodhicharya-Avatara,* an explanation is given that is based on the nonconceptual mind. In this case, conventional truth is any phenomenon that is realized as having a slightly dualistic appearance, whereas ultimate truth is one that is realized by the ultimate mind and doesn't have the dualistic appearance.

Generally, when we talk about having dualistic appearances, we mean many things. For example, dualistic appearance sometimes refers to perception of conventional phenomena, sometimes to the truly existent nature of a phenomenon and sometimes to an appearance of the generic image of a phenomenon.

What is the etymological meaning of the Two Truths? The term "conventional truth" is so used because it holds true for a concealing or obscuring mind (in the sense that it is a concealing mind by its mode of existence). It is seemingly true for a particular mind, and that particular mind sees it as ignorance (and ignorance signifies an obscuring mind). Such a mind lacks knowledge of that particular object, and sees it as true. That is why it is called "conventional truth" and not "ultimate truth."

If we follow the conventional truth according to the Sanskrit tradition, then the word "conventional" can have different meanings. The word sometimes means *samvritisatya,* which in itself can have different meanings. Sometimes it can refer to that which obscures the quality or to the conventional thing. It also means something that is dependent on some other base. Thus, "conventional" here refers to an obscuring mind that is the true grasping ignorance.

Conventional truth has different classifications. It signifies that the real mode of existence of a particular phenomenon and the way it appears do not coincide. Therefore it cannot be true, but based on the view of the worldly people, it can be classified into two categories: real conventional truth and unreal conventional truth. Based on the worldly view, there are two classes. For example, a person in a dream is unreal conventional truth, whereas an actual person is a real conventional truth. It is thus from the worldly point of view that the two classes are distinguished, and not because of its real mode of existence.

Regarding the ultimate truth, different masters of the Madhyamika school interpret it differently. To some, the term "ultimate truth," or the word "ultimate," means the real nature of phenomena. The real nature of phenomena is supreme and something that one should know. One must try and realize this supreme reality. This is why it is called "ultimate." The word "ultimate" can also be referred to in two ways. Sometimes it may refer to the object of negation, something that is to be refuted. At other times it may refer to the wisdom that one should generate. If we use this word with reference to the object of designation, there is no phenomenon that exists ultimately. But if we refer to an object that can be ultimately realized by a wisdom consciousness, it is an existent phenomenon. If the object of refutation is a particular thing that exists, then we should be able to find it through the wisdom consciousness. And if it is something that is realized and understood by the wisdom consciousness, it is not necessary that it should exist by itself. For example, the emptiness or suchness of that ultimate truth is perceived by the wisdom consciousness.

If we take up a particular phenomenon and analyze its nature, in the end it cannot be found. For example, if we first analyze the flower to discover its ultimate nature and its reality, we will discover the emptiness or inherent nature of the emptiness, which itself cannot be found. However, we will find the emptiness of the emptiness.

In the sutras, the ultimate truth has been classified into twenty or sometimes sixteen types, but it can be precisely divided into two subsections: emptiness of the person and emptiness of the phenomena—or selflessness of the person and selflessness of the phenomena.

So, as I explained earlier, the word "ultimate" interpreted from the tantric point of view refers sometimes to the subjective mind or consciousness. At times it can also refer to the object. Generally, it has three meanings: the object, the wisdom consciousness and the effect of it. When we follow the tantric tradition, it has a different meaning. The different texts, particularly the tantric texts, use the word "ultimate" in various ways, each having its own connotation. Hence, it is very important to understand the meaning of the word "ultimate" in its different contexts. Otherwise, one can be confused and lost. When we use the terms "conventional" and "ultimate truth" in general, they cover both the tantric and the sutric levels and encompass the entire body of knowledge. But when we refer to the tantric tradition, they do not necessarily cover the entire body of knowledge. They sometimes refer only to the path.

30

Who finds the emptiness?
I think there must be someone here who will find
emptiness. You are bound to find it if you practice
very sincerely in your daily life, and particularly
when you encounter a certain object that creates
a strong emotion such as attachment or hatred,
or is the face of strong ego. During that moment,
if you carry out a very careful investigation, if you
analyze and examine the mode of apprehension
of the mind, the way things appear in the mind,
you find that at that time, the object appears to be
very strong and forceful. It appears to be very
solid and independent. For example, when feelings of hatred develop, the object appears as 100
percent negative. But that is actually an exaggeration. Nothing is 100 percent negative. However,
during that moment, due to one's own mental attitude, it appears to be so. That moment is the
best opportunity and the right time to analyze
the real nature and its appearances. Then you see
emptiness with its logical reasons and proofs and
discover that things are relative. For example, by
analyzing the causes of a particular phenomenon,
and using reasons like "diamond sliver" and so on,
and further by analyzing the entity of that particular phenomenon and whether it exists singly or

in many parts. Also, by analyzing the effect of a particular phenomenon, whether existent or nonexistent, and finally, the logical reasoning of the dependent nature or dependent arising. So, if you analyze carefully, although it is difficult to realize fully, you can feel that there is something. That is quite certain.

Realization of emptiness is very, very important because when we try to analyze the real nature of any particular phenomenon, we find that the real nature is emptiness or lack of inherent existence. It is possible to think that emptiness is truly existent. It is important to realize the emptiness of emptiness because emptiness itself has no independent existence. It is also dependent on something. For example, if we take a casual look at any particular phenomenon and its real nature, that particular object will seem to be more powerful than the emptiness of that particular phenomenon since we cannot explain something like emptiness without depending upon that particular phenomenon. In other words, emptiness is a particular quality or aspect of a phenomenon. For any quality there must be some basis. Thus *shunya* also becomes a part of some thing—the quality of some thing.

Consciousness is also in the nature of emptiness. There is a simple reason for it. Emptiness means the absence of independent existence or self-existence. The Sanskrit word *pratityasamuta-pada* means "dependent arising." "Dependent" because it is dependent on others and is not of absolute nature. "Arising" means something that has happened due to other factors. In a way, it is something like zero. Without a zero, it is impossible to count. Because things are related, "empty" here means "like something empty." Therefore, if its basic nature is something, everything is possible. That basis leads to this absence of absolute nature.

Generally, when we talk about something untrue in the worldly sense, it is not because it is untrue in the face of a wisdom consciousness, but because it is untrue at the worldly level. Thus, you have the sense of the untruth and the unreality of the conditional truth. If someone takes interest, there is clearly a relation. For example, in daily life, our experience of pain and pleasure depends very much on our mental attitude. However, once you realize the conventional and the ultimate levels of truth, it is very helpful to reduce mental exaggeration. Realization of the Two Truths is also very helpful in making your mind stable.

We simply accept the good and the bad due to

realization of the deeper nature. If we are able to acquire a sound understanding of the real nature of the ultimate and the conventional truth, we will encounter external phenomena with a balanced perspective. However, before understanding the real nature of the Two Truths, we tend to exaggerate phenomena. Our mind is one solid entity; at least it appears like that. But in reality, there are many different kinds of mind. The human mind is especially sophisticated. Therefore, in order to achieve peace of mind, true Buddhist training or technique reduces mental unrest and increases mental happiness and mental peace. There are many different ways of achieving peace and reducing anxiety. Knowledge about the Two Truths is one of them. Generally speaking, the spiritual practice is like a stabilizer. Peace is similar.

Can you say something about good and bad?
Good and bad from the Buddhist point of view are relative terms and depend on other factors. Under certain circumstances something may be good, but under other circumstances, it becomes bad. So there is no absolute. We have to judge according to particular circumstances. Generally, we can say that any action or any factor that

brings us happiness or satisfaction is good; anything that brings us unhappiness or pain is bad. So the ultimate decision about good and bad is based on experience and feeling. Our mind has the final word.

I think it is mental tranquillity that allows us relaxation and happiness. This holds true for everyone. Another practice is that of altruism. As things are interdependent, our own satisfaction, or happiness, depends largely on others. If other people, including animals, are satisfied and show happiness or some kind of a positive response, we will be satisfied. Therefore, the practice of altruism is the key factor.

The first half of my lecture was about the basis of the Two Truths and the Four Noble Truths. I shall now talk about how to implement and utilize them in our daily life or daily practice.

There are two ways of approaching the Four Noble Truths. One is to think more about the Two Truths; it will allow you to understand the Four Noble Truths better. In the second case, think about the Four Noble Truths; then on the question of cessation—*nirodha*—the explanation of the Two Truths can be made. The first Noble Truth is the realization of suffering nature. If our life is good and consists of permanent happiness, there is no need to think about other complicated things. But our life is not so simple and does not have such a nature.

In order to know life's suffering nature, we need to understand the three kinds of suffering. The first is the suffering of suffering. This manifests itself in the form of, say, headaches and pains and is applicable even to animals. There is a way to escape or overcome this kind of suffering temporarily. The second is suffering of change. These are the experiences we usually regard as pleasurable. For example, when we get something new, for the first few days we are very excited and feel very happy. However, after a while the same article creates some sort of dissatisfaction or frustration.

We may feel very close to something very beautiful at first, but later on the same thing may appear ugly and not so good. Moreover, we may want to get rid of it. It is very natural for people who remain in a small village or in a remote place to desire a more attractive life in another place, a bigger city or a bigger country. And sometimes, people who are in a big city often prefer to be in a rural or quiet place. Desires are always changing. This is the second category of suffering: the suffering of change.

There are different interpretations of the third suffering—conditioned suffering. One interpretation is that our body is under the influence of ignorance. There are different kinds of ignorance. One is mere ignorance, that is, you simply don't know something. Another kind of ignorance is one that makes us see phenomena in a perverted or wrong manner. This kind of ignorance is the real seed of trouble or the seed of suffering. So when ignorance is a troublemaker, it should be eliminated. It is worthwhile trying to eliminate it. If suffering is something that can be eliminated, it is useful, then, to see suffering for what it is and not be afraid of it, dislike it or get frustrated about it. Now the crucial question is whether there is cessation or not. Here we naturally have to bring in consciousness. There are two separate phenomena: matter and consciousness. If we view a flower or our body in terms of particles or molecules, they are similar in substance and follow the same system. The difference, however, is that flowers do not have consciousness as human beings do. Besides these physical particles there is something that we call consciousness. When bodies or particles combine with consciousness, we have sentient beings. Then, a feeling of "I" is developed.

When it comes to the different levels of consciousness, when we are awake, we have one level of consciousness. While we are dreaming, another slightly deeper level of consciousness is at work. When we are in deep sleep without dreams, we are in a state of even deeper consciousness or mind. When we faint or when breathing stops, during that period consciousness becomes more subtle. Usually people refer to this state as being "unconscious," but in fact, consciousness or mind becomes deeper then. The deepest consciousness or mind, however, occurs only when we die.

The grosser mind depends very much on physical organs like the brain or different nervous systems. The deeper the consciousness, the more independent it becomes from the body. Therefore, when physical functions completely stop, the most subtle mind becomes active. At the time of death there is the normal process of separation of the subtle consciousness and the body. The practitioner who has a certain practice of yoga or certain meditations can voluntarily dissociate or separate the two. Through meditation, you can also control blood circulation, breathing and other physical functions. Eventually, if you intensify your training, there is a possibility of making this separation. Through the practice of transference of consciousness, we can make this separation. However, it is very dangerous for the beginner, as he or she may be able to separate the body and mind, but not be able to reunite it. It is much easier to separate than to reunite.

Discussions with neuroscientists and neurobiologists reveal knowledge about the brain and its functions as well. Perhaps there is scope for further discussion along these lines. Through experience we can say that there is an aspect of mind—especially energy—that controls the nervous system. As I mentioned earlier, physical health is highly connected with mental health. There are already experiments of curing illness through meditation. When we talk about ignorance, we refer to some fault or defect of consciousness, or the defective quality of consciousness. In order to decrease these negative qualities of the mind and to deal with this kind of a mind, changes occur in the nature of doubt. This kind of transformation influences cognition, and finally we are able to get the nonconceptual direct perception.

Thus, if one is to eliminate this kind of defective mind, it is important to understand the nature and the transformation of the mind. First try to examine the state of mind. Sometimes one experiences a different kind of consciousness and wild thoughts. This is because of the presence of too many conceptual thoughts that obscure phenomena. The real nature of the mind is obstructed—as when you add color to clear glass, it is very difficult to see the clear glass. Therefore, usually if we try to clear the grosser level of consciousness and wild thoughts, we get a glimpse of the real nature of mind. At that stage we feel the empty nature of mind. This is one technique by which to realize it. Here, when I say nature, it is not the ultimate nature, but the conventional nature of mind. Early in the morning, when you are already awake but your mind is not yet fully active, sometimes you experience clear and colorless thoughts. So the very nature of mind is like something that is white and can absorb other colors. It is something neutral, not something good, but something pure. Then there are other thoughts that accompany this pure mind. For example, nobody can remain angry all the time. As long as consciousness and awareness exist, even if a person is very short-tempered, there are moments when he or she has no temper. In the case of attachment, no matter how strong it may be, the basic nature of the mind shows that it can be removed. Depending upon the external and internal factors, attachment either increases or

decreases. So there is a possibility to reduce attachment.

Now the question is whether there is a possibility of reducing these thoughts. In order to do
this, you have to know the mode of their existence, and the way they appear to us. In general,
we make a categorical distinction between the
quality of a particular object and its parts. And
when we talk about an object, its quality and its
conceptuality, we have distinct qualities in mind
although when we talk about an object and its effect, then they are two different phenomena. If
this is the real mode of existence, we should be
able to find it when we realize it, but it cannot be
found. Therefore, if we eliminate the parts, we
will never be able to find the real object that
causes them.

This, however, suits the conventional mode of
existence, and is not possible for the ultimate
mode of existence. In general, if we try to find
the basis of designation for all phenomena, it cannot be found. On the worldly level, we can search
to some extent, but beyond that, if we split the
phenomena in parts and try to find it, we cannot.
For example, take the case of "I." Usually we
think that "I" is an owner or something belonging
to that owner. So it is supposed to have a separate

identity besides the body and mind. In general, when we talk about "I," we have a wrong sense of "I" as being the possessor of mind and body. To illustrate: there is a person with a defective body or mind. If someone comes and says, "I will give you a better body and better peace of mind," then he or she will immediately generate a consciousness willing to accept it. This clearly indicates that we have the wrong notion that "I" is separate from the aggregate of the consciousness and the mind. Yet if we examine our body and mind, there is nothing left. Of course, there is an "I." If there were no "I," then there would be no "other." If there was no "other," then there would be no point in practicing altruism. So there is definitely an "I" and the "other." However, the usual explanation is that there is an "I" but it is simply designated on the combination of the body and mind. Every phenomenon, thus, is designated on the combination of its parts, which, if we investigate, we cannot find. But if we deny these things because we cannot find them and say that a person is nonexistent, it contradicts our daily experience. Our experience clearly shows that the person is existent and not nonexistent. If we deny his or her existence, we fall into the extreme of annihilation. Although the person is very much existent, the existence is only conventional. It does not exist independently. This clearly annihilates the extreme of permanence.

When we talk about a person being designated and dependent on something, it eliminates the two extremes: the extreme of total nonexistence and the extreme of permanence. Therefore, we call it the Madhyamika or middle way. When we talk about the realization of the middle way or middle view, it means things are neither totally nonexistent nor do they have an independent existence. Phenomena appear to us as existing on their own without depending on anything, but this is not the case. They only have an existence dependent upon other phenomena. They are only designated by the mind. So the realization of such an understanding is the realization of the view of the Madhyamika.

It is worthwhile at this juncture to examine the generation of anger and attachment in the light of the above view. It is very clear that when we generate anger and attachment, that particular object of anger and attachment appears as something that exists independently, as something solid. It is very clear that when strong anger or strong attachment is developed, the object appears as independent and something 100 percent negative or positive. But with the passage of time, when anger and attachment are reduced or disappear—your feeling toward the same person will be different. For example, when a couple marries, both parties may seem 100 percent beautiful and good to one another. This is mainly due to their projection owing to attachment. When there is some trouble, the strong emotion decreases. But when the trouble or anger disappears, the real mode of the person begins to appear.

It is very clear that when we generate the negative mind, its root is the wrong mode of grasping at phenomena. This true grasping at phenomena and the consciousness perceiving the lack of true existence of phenomena are contradictory in their modes of apprehension. These two consciousnesses are directed toward the same objects, but their modes of apprehension are different. Thus these two consciousnesses oppose each other. The only difference between these two consciousnesses is that the consciousness perceiving the lack of true existence has a valid support and valid foundation, whereas the other does not.

There is a possibility of eliminating all negative thoughts. As time goes by, and the deeper the meditation coupled with analytical meditation, negative emotions and thoughts can be eventually eliminated. This state of mind having eliminated negative emotions is what we usually call nirvana, moksha or cessation. Cessation does not mean the cessation of our consciousness or cessation of oneself; it means cessation of negative emotions. In the Buddhist school of thought there are different interpretations of moksha. For example, the Vaibhashika school of thought believes that when you achieve true cessation, *nirodha* or moksha, there is no more consciousness, no more psychophysical aggregates, or *skhandha*, and no more being. However, as Nāgājuna says, "If that is the case, then there is no being to achieve it." Thus we cannot say that there is a being who will achieve nirvana, because when nirvana happens, there is no more being; and if there is a being, there can be no nirvana. The very nature of consciousness is pure, so there is no reason to cease or end it. In Madhyamika and Cittamatra philosophy, nirvana definitely exists, but the being with self-identity also exists. Even in the case of Buddhahood, a Buddha with his or her own individual identity exists. For me, moksha is the complete cessation of the mind, the cessation of "I." I would prefer samsara to nirvana because in samsara there is life and experience. I think this is better than just nothingness.

People get the impression that cessation, or nirvana, is nothingness, and that all feelings, consciousness and things dissolve in emptiness. There is nothing left. That is wrong. Actually, nirvana is the completely purified state of one's own mind. It is the ultimate nature of mind that has removed all afflictive emotions.

It is our responsibility to feel "yes, there is a way and something worthwhile to achieve." So we should try to investigate the suffering nature, and on getting frustrated with that we should develop the feeling of renunciation in order to achieve nirvana, which is permanent liberation. If we think only of the first two of the Four Noble Truths without properly thinking about the latter two, it would not work or serve their purpose. Sometimes people might be intolerant of the practitioner's passivity, inactivity and pessimism if he or she thinks only about the first two truths. Thus, strike a balance and try to understand the two negative truths as well as the two positive truths. You will then have a clear purpose or goal, and a better understanding and realization about their nature. Automatically you will feel frustration toward negative thoughts and that is very important. Actually, our real enemy—the real troublemaker or destroyer of happiness—is within ourselves. For example, anger, hatred, attachment and extreme greed are the destroyers of inner peace, whereas the external enemy, no matter how powerful, simply cannot destroy inner peace. If someone is mentally calm and peaceful, it does not matter even if that person is surrounded by hostility, because the person will feel very little disturbance. On the other hand, if you are mentally unhappy, restless or disturbed, even if you are surrounded by best friends or the best facilities, you will not get peace and happiness. So inner peace and the source of it are the inevitable end or result of a tranquil and settled mind. Thus, the inevitable and ultimate cause of mental calmness and happiness cannot be any external factor.

The ultimate source of mental peace can be destroyed only by one's anger and negative thoughts. A wise person will not allow anger or hatred to manifest themselves because nobody wants unhappiness or suffering. If you want to attain happiness, you must take care of the ultimate source of happiness. You must practice love, kindness, and try to reduce your anger. These are not religious matters but they concern our daily happiness.

At the ordinary level, when negative thoughts of anger and attachment arise, these appear effective and helpful. For instance, when we are facing a problem, losing or failing, anger comes as a protector or supporter. Anger tells us not to fear and allows itself to be expressed. An angry person is almost mad and uses harsh words or indulges in harmful physical actions and so on. In a way, anger gives us a boldness or force. Similarly, when attachment arises, it comes as our best and dearest friend. Thus, unless we analyze very sincerely and seriously, it is very difficult to realize these negative thoughts and their negative and false quality.

When anger dominates our mind, we sometimes use harsh and unpleasant words. But when anger subsides, we feel embarrassed to withdraw our words and so we avoid meeting the person we have had differences with. This shows that basically we do not want to use harsh words but anger at that time made us lose all control. Therefore, anger is an enemy and is not useful or reliable. In some other cases, we need a strong countermeasure against anger. When something happens, analyze and thoroughly investigate the situation. If it needs an effective countermeasure, take it without anger, as any action motivated by anger will be ineffective. Also, in many cases, decisions taken under the influence of anger are usually found to be wrong. Hatred and anger make us lose our appetite and sleep, and we suffer mentally. The enemy actually feels happy seeing us depressed. On the other hand, however, if we remain calm and in a very happy mood, the enemy is not able to feel any satisfaction. Furthermore, anger really destroys our sense of judgment that can discern long- and short-term consequences. Having an enemy is useful because it gives us the opportunity to practice patience and tolerance. This practice is highly necessary for the development of genuine compassion and love.

We cannot learn real patience and tolerance from a guru or a friend. They can be practiced only when we come in contact with someone who creates unpleasant experiences. According to Shantideva, enemies are really good for us as we can learn a lot from them and build our inner strength. The practice of love and compassion is not a religious practice or a sacred thing, but a question of survival. In terms of humanity, I think the economy is facing a global crisis and there is, of course, the question of world peace. In every field the important factor is compassion and a good heart. Here we have to distinguish between love and compassion. Usually people are impatient in love, as love is mixed or polluted with attachment. The indication of such a pollution is that our love is dependent on how the other person responds to us. For example, if someone is very close to us, and something distasteful happens, our attitude changes immediately and the love disappears. However, there is another kind of love that is genuine, where one realizes that the other person is like oneself who wants happiness and does not want suffering, and who has every right to overcome the suffering and achieve happiness. On that basis, a genuine love and kindness is developed and that remains in the relationship.

When we talk about the importance of love and kindness, we refer to genuine love, and not the love and kindness that are greatly influenced by ignorance. Sometimes people say that when anger arises, it is better to express it rather than hide or suppress it. Of course there are different levels of anger. The first and foremost thing is to realize the negativity of anger and hatred. Once you are convinced of that, you naturally try to distance yourself from it. Yet if strong anger arises, and is difficult to suppress, just try to forget about the object of anger. Take, for example, my own practice and my own experience. I am from Amdo, in the northeastern part of Tibet. People from these areas are generally regarded as being very short-tempered. When I was young, even I had that trait. As time passed, I practiced these things to subdue my mind. My anger has reduced greatly. On certain occasions, anger or irritation arise but they disappear quickly. And I have hardly any feeling of hatred.

Thus, it is through practice that you can bring about your inner development. There is a possibility of change. In order to change, we must first change ourselves. If we don't change, nothing will change, and expecting others to change is then quite unrealistic. So the human mind is always changing; and if you make some effort in the right direction, ultimately, mental changes will occur and you can get an enormous amount of peace and happiness without any pain or expense. Peace and happiness must be developed within oneself. As Buddha says, "You are your own master. One's future entirely depends on oneself. Nobody else can take care of one's future life and the present rests on one's own shoulders."

3D

Is it possible to be completely free from the presence of negative ego or is this just a myth?
Since defects and faults are not inherent qualities of the mind, it is possible that this fault can be eliminated.

If we remove mind and body, silent awareness appears. This awareness is the same in all sentient beings. This is the essence of realization of self-identity. Please comment.

In general, the continuity of the mind remains; therefore it is not possible to eliminate the mind and body and then achieve self-identity. As I mentioned earlier, according to Mahayana teachings, even at the stage of Enlightenment, wisdom is manifested in the individual self.

Please explain the emptiness of ultimate phenomena like death and karma.

When we talk about emptiness, regardless of any phenomenon, emptiness means the lack of inherent existence of that particular phenomenon. Action (karma) and death are also phenomena, but not ultimate truths. Their ultimate nature is *shunyata*. It is important to know about death and karma. Karma is action with motivation, and a certain mental as well as physical action is involved.

An action is bound to have a result. In Buddhism, karma also means action, but here you have the long- and short-term consequences. For example, we may say that there is a certain negative motivation behind the action of anger. With that motivation comes some kind of rough physical action and the negative mental action creates a negative and unpleasant atmosphere. This is a short-term consequence, and during that moment that action leaves the imprint on the consciousness. This imprint is left on the "I" and is carried by the continuity of the mind, or the "I," and one starts experiencing the effects as and when the imprint is faced with external conditions.

When we talk about death, it relates to the absorption of the subtle minds. A subtler explanation can be found in the eight stages of absorption. This is actually a special subject that one should study.

Anger is the truth. It must coexist with happiness; then why should one control it?

If you ask doctors, they will tell you that we can do without anger in our lives. You will get more pleasure and happiness if you try to minimize anger. So, the valid question really is whether anger *can* be reduced or not.

I do not understand how attachment causes suffering because I get strength from attachment, especially when I am disturbed.

Attachment as a cause of suffering is related to

the third category of suffering: pervasive compositional suffering. Anger is directly connected to it as anger brings us the first category of suffering, whereas attachment brings us the second and third. This body of ours exists because of attachment. So you see, through attachment and anger, the different kinds of suffering are introduced; thus attachment is actually the basis of anger.

Please explain a simple technique to reduce anger.
A more analytical examination of the real shortcomings of anger will help. Anger destroys one's peace of mind and creates further trouble. If you look at world history, you can see that all destruction, human misery and suffering were mainly caused by hatred and anger. The glorious stories about good revolved around altruism. Thus, you will realize that anger is really worthless. If someone accepts the theory of rebirth and karma (cause and effect), other methods can be used to reduce anger. Family problems are most often created by anger. So you can learn from the experiences of others.

When the environment is polluted, is it possible to generate a pure state of mind?
There is a definite relationship between the ex-

ternal environment and the mind. Owing to pollution, the brain does not function well; there is a kind of dullness. But it is not impossible to have a pure mind even amid a polluted environment.

What is emptiness?
Emptiness is emptiness; the answer is not easy. One has to go into more detail and depth. It takes months and years before you arrive at an understanding of it.

Constitution Club Lawns, 1988

INDEX